Substance Abuse Issues
Among Families
in Diverse Populations

Substance Abuse Issues Among Families in Diverse Populations has been co-published simultaneously as *Journal of Family Social Work*, Volume 4, Number 4 2000.

The *Journal of Family Social Work* Monographic *"Separates"*

(formerly the *Journal of Social Work & Human Sexuality* series)*

For information on previous issues of the *Journal of Social Work & Human Sexuality* series, please contact:
The Haworth Press, Inc., 10 Alice Street, Binghamton, NY 13904-1580 USA.

Below is a list of "separates," which in serials librarianship means a special issue simultaneously published as a special journal issue or double-issue *and* as a "separate" hardbound monograph. (This is a format which we also call a "DocuSerial.")

"Separates" are published because specialized libraries or professionals may wish to purchase a specific thematic issue by itself in a format which can be separately cataloged and shelved, as opposed to purchasing the journal on an on-going basis. Faculty members may also more easily consider a "separate" for classroom adoption.

"Separates" are carefully classified separately with the major book jobbers so that the journal tie-in can be noted on new book order slips to avoid duplicate purchasing.

You may wish to visit Haworth's website at . . .

http://www.haworthpressinc.com

. . . to search our online catalog for complete tables of contents of these separates and related publications.

You may also call 1-800-HAWORTH (outside US/Canada: 607-722-5857), or Fax 1-800-895-0582 (outside US/Canada: 607-771-0012), or e-mail at:

getinfo@haworthpressinc.com

Substance Abuse Issues Among Families in Diverse Populations, edited by Jorge Delva, PhD (Vol. 4, No. 4, 2000). *Discusses a variety of substance abuse issues including drug testing of welfare applicants as a requirement for benefits, parental substance abuse in African American and Latino families, and the perspectives of long-time Al-Anon members.*

Social Work and the Family Unit, edited by David J. Ludwig, PhD, MDiv (Vol. 4, No. 3, 2000). *Offers therapists methods and suggestions for helping clients focus on problems within relationships and provides techniques and examples for conducting more successful and productive sessions.*

The Family, Spirituality, and Social Work, edited by Dorothy S. Becvar, MSW, PhD (Vol. 2, No. 4, 1998). *"This groundbreaking text is an evocative excursion into the realm of 'spirituality' within the domain of human services and treatment." (Marcia D. Brown-Standridge, ACSW, PhD, private practice, Terre Haute, Indiana)*

Cross-Cultural Practice with Couples and Families, edited by Philip M. Brown, PhD, LCSW, and John S. Shalett, MSW, BCSW (Vol. 2, No. 1/2, 1997). *"An excellent resource for practitioners and educators alike. It is an eye-opener and a first step in the process of understanding true diversity and cultural sensitivity." (Multicultural Review)*

Sexuality and Disabilities: A Guide for Human Service Practitioners, edited by Romel W. Mackelprang, DSW, MSW, and Deborah Valentine, PhD, MSW (Vol. 8, No. 2, 1993).* *"Emphasizes the need for individualized counseling in a supportive, educational context." (Science Books and Films)*

Adolescent Sexuality: New Challenges for Social Work, edited by Paula Allen-Meares, PhD, MSW, and Constance Hoenk Shapiro, PhD, MSW (Vol. 8, No. 1, 1989).* *"This is a valuable and wide-ranging look at the vital, complex, and very specific issues of adolescent sexuality and their implications for social work and social workers." (Paul H. Ephross, PhD, Professor, School of Social Work and Community Planning, University of Maryland at Baltimore)*

Treatment of Sex Offenders in Social Work and Mental Health Settings, edited by John S. Wodarski, PhD, and Daniel Whitaker, MSW (Vol. 7, No. 2, 1989).* *"The editors, besides contributing their own share of expertise, surrounded themselves with scientific experts who clearly enunciated their experiences in research design, data, conclusions, and applications." (Journal of the American Association of Psychiatric Administrators)*

The Sexually Unusual: Guide to Understanding and Helping, edited by Dennis M. Dailey, DSW (Vol. 7, No. 1, 1989).* *"If you want to know what you don't know about human sexual behavior, I challenge you to read this book, which is timely, cogent, and without a doubt, superior to any other book on this subject."* (Arthur Herman, MSW, Chief Social Worker and Associate Director, Center for Sexual Health, Menninger Clinic, The Menninger Foundation, Topeka, Kansas)

Sociological Aspects of Sexually Transmitted Diseases, edited by Margaret Rodway and Marianne Wright (Vol. 6, No. 2, 1988).* *"The most comprehensive resource guide on the topic of sexually transmitted diseases. It belongs in all the libraries of helping professionals and students, and is an up-to-date volume on an emerging issue in the field of human sexuality."* (Professor Benjamin Schlesinger, Faculty of Social Work, University of Toronto, Canada; Author of Sexual Behavior in Canada (University of Toronto Press))

Infertility and Adoption: A Guide for Social Work Practice, edited by Deborah Valentine (Vol. 6, No. 1, 1988).* *"Provides educators and practitioners with a rich compendium of information that will not only enhance their understanding of the dynamics involved in assessing and treating individuals and families presenting with concerns around fertility and adoption, but also provide an expanded context that takes into consideration program and policy issues."* (Sadye L. Logan, DSW, Associate Professor, University of Kansas, School of Social Welfare)

Intimate Relationships: Some Social Work Perspectives on Love, edited by Wendell Ricketts, BA, and Harvey Gochros, PhD (Vol. 5, No. 2, 1987).* *Insightful perspectives on the social worker's role in the counseling of clients who have problems with different kinds of love.*

Adolescent Sexualities: Overviews and Principles of Intervention, edited by Paula Allen-Meares, PhD, and David A. Shore, PhD (Vol. 5, No. 1, 1986).* *"The collection moves beyond many other articles and books by offering practical solutions and ideas for individuals working with adolescents."* (SIECUS Report)

Human Sexuality, Ethnoculture, and Social Work, edited by Larry Lister, DSW (Vol. 4, No. 3, 1987).* *A valuable work providing basic cultural information within the context of human sexuality of several ethnocultural groups.*

Social Work Practice in Sexual Problems, edited by James Gripton, DSW, and Mary Valentich, PhD (Vol. 4, No. 1/2, 1986).* *"Serves as a valuable resource since it appears to encompass the major areas related to sexual problems."* (Shankar A. Yelaja, DSW, Dean, Faculty of Social Work, Wilfrid Laurier University)

Feminist Perspectives on Social Work and Human Sexuality, edited by Mary Valentich, PhD, and James Gripton, PhD, DSW (Vol. 3, No. 2/3, 1985).* *"Contains a powerful and unnerving message for educators, clinicians, and students. . . . important and useful . . . a valued addition to professional as well as academic libraries."* (Canadian Social Work Review)

Homosexuality and Social Work, edited by Robert Schoenberg, ACSW, and Richard S. Goldberg, MSS (Vol. 2, No. 2/3, 1984).* *"Packed with useful information on the special problems of both gay and lesbian clients. . . . A treasured resource for nurses, counselors, physicians, and other helping professionals."* (Contemporary Sociology)

Human Sexuality in Medical Social Work, edited by Larry Lister, DSW, and David A. Shore, PhD (Vol. 2, No. 1, 1984).* *"Excellently researched and written. . . . The role of the social worker as a member of the health care team is very well highlighted. . . . makes a valuable contribution to the counseling community."* (Journal of Sex Education & Therapy)

Social Work and Child Sexual Abuse, edited by Jon R. Conte, PhD, and David A. Shore, PhD (Vol. 1, No. 1/2, 1982).* *"This volume is a solid one, which contains a wealth of knowledge for the helping professional."* (The Canadian Journal of Human Sexuality)

Substance Abuse Issues Among Families in Diverse Populations

Jorge Delva, PhD
Editor

Substance Abuse Issues Among Families in Diverse Populations has been co-published simultaneously as *Journal of Family Social Work*, Volume 4, Number 4 2000.

The Haworth Press, Inc.
New York • London • Oxford

Substance Abuse Issues Among Families in Diverse Populations
has been co-published simultaneously as *Journal of Family Social Work*™, Volume 4, Number 4 2000.

The development, preparation, and publication of this work has been undertaken with great care. However, the publisher, employees, editors, and agents of The Haworth Press and all imprints of The Haworth Press, Inc., including The Haworth Medical Press® and Pharmaceutical Products Press®, are not responsible for any errors contained herein or for consequences that may ensue from use of materials or information contained in this work. Opinions expressed by the author(s) are not necessarily those of The Haworth Press, Inc.

The Haworth Press, Inc., 10 Alice Street, Binghamton, NY 13904-1580 USA

Cover design by Thomas J. Mayshock Jr.

Library of Congress Cataloging-in-Publication Data

Substance abuse issues among families in diverse populations / Jorge Delva, editor.
    p. cm.
    "Substance abuse issues among families in diverse populations, has been co-published simultaneously as Journal of family social work, volume 4, number 4, 2000."
    Includes bibliographical references and index.
    ISBN 0-7890-1194-8 (alk. paper) – ISBN 0-7890-1195-6 (alk. paper)
    1. Minorities–Drug use. 2. Minorities–Alcohol use. 3. Family social work. 4. Social work with minorities. I. Delva, Jorge.

HV5824.E85 S83 2000
362.29'089–dc21

00-031968

INDEXING & ABSTRACTING

Contributions to this publication are selectively indexed or abstracted in print, electronic, online, or CD-ROM version(s) of the reference tools and information services listed below. This list is current as of the copyright date of this publication. See the end of this section for additional notes.

- *Abstracts in Anthropology*
- *Abstracts in Social Gerontology: Current Literature on Aging*
- *Abstracts of Research in Pastoral Care & Counseling*
- *Applied Social Sciences Index & Abstracts (ASSIA) (Online: ASSI via Data-Star) (CDRom: ASSIA Plus)*
- *BUBL Information Service: An Internet-based Information Service for the UK higher education community <URL: http://bubl.ac.uk/>*
- *Cambridge Scientific Abstracts (Health & Safety Science Abstracts/Risk Abstracts)*
- *caredata CD: the social & community care database*
- *Child Development Abstracts & Bibliography*
- *CINAHL (Cumulative Index to Nursing & Allied Health Literature), in print, also on CD-ROM from CD PLUS, EBSCO, and SilverPlatter, and online from CDP Online (formerly BRS), Data-Star, and PaperChase*
- *CNPIEC Reference Guide: Chinese National Directory of Foreign Periodicals*
- *Criminal Justice Abstracts*
- *Educational Administration Abstracts (EAA)*
- *ERIC Clearinghouse on Counseling and Student Services (ERIC/CASS)*
- *Family Studies Database (online and CD/ROM)*
- *Family Violence & Sexual Assault Bulletin*
- *FINDEX <www.publist.com>*
- *Human Resources Abstracts (HRA)*
- *IBZ International Bibliography of Periodical Literature*
- *Index to Periodical Articles Related to Law*
- *Linguistics and Language Behavior Abstracts (LLBA) <www.csa.com>*
- *Mental Health Abstracts (online through DIALOG)*

(continued)

- *National Criminal Justice Reference Service*
- *PASCAL, c/o Institute de L'Information Scientifique et Technique*
- *Periodica Islamica*
- *Psychological Abstracts (PsycINFO)*
- *Referativnyi Zhurnal (Abstracts Journal of the All-Russian Institute of Scientific and Technical Information)*
- *Sage Family Studies Abstracts (SFSA)*
- *Social Services Abstracts <www.csa.com>*
- *Social Work Abstracts*
- *Sociological Abstracts (SA) <www.csa.com>*
- *Studies on Women Abstracts*
- *Violence and Abuse Abstracts: A Review of Current Literature on Interpersonal Violence (VAA)*

Special Bibliographic Notes related to special journal issues (separates) and indexing/abstracting:

- indexing/abstracting services in this list will also cover material in any "separate" that is co-published simultaneously with Haworth's special thematic journal issue or DocuSerial. Indexing/abstracting usually covers material at the article/chapter level.
- monographic co-editions are intended for either non-subscribers or libraries which intend to purchase a second copy for their circulating collections.
- monographic co-editions are reported to all jobbers/wholesalers/approval plans. The source journal is listed as the "series" to assist the prevention of duplicate purchasing in the same manner utilized for books-in-series.
- to facilitate user/access services all indexing/abstracting services are encouraged to utilize the co-indexing entry note indicated at the bottom of the first page of each article/chapter/contribution.
- this is intended to assist a library user of any reference tool (whether print, electronic, online, or CD-ROM) to locate the monographic version if the library has purchased this version but not a subscription to the source journal.
- individual articles/chapters in any Haworth publication are also available through the Haworth Document Delivery Service (HDDS).

Substance Abuse Issues Among Families in Diverse Populations

CONTENTS

ABOUT THE EDITOR

Jorge Delva, PhD, is Assistant Professor in the School of Social Work at Florida State University. A native of Chile, he received his doctorate in social welfare from the University of Hawaii where he learned to truly appreciate diversity and the important role that culture plays in a person's development, health and functioning. His interest in cultures led him to study Mandarin, Japanese, and some Samoan. Recently, Dr. Delva completed a two-year postdoctoral fellowship in drug epidemiology at The Johns Hopkins University funded by the National Institute on Drug Abuse. While at Hopkins, he assisted with the development of school-based drug surveys in several countries in Central America. His most recent projects involve evaluating the effectiveness of Florida's substance abuse treatment services and studying the occurrence of drug use as a multi-level phenomenon among individuals of racial and ethnic minorities using data from the National Household Survey on Drug Abuse.

Introduction

This volume has the pleasure of presenting a series of articles that discuss the problem of substance use and abuse that our society faces today. The articles discuss this problem and the effect it has on families from a variety of perspectives. The first article is entitled "Conditional Welfare: A Family Social Work Perspective on Mandatory Drug Testing." This article discusses the pros and cons of drug testing welfare recipients and discusses the social work implications of this policy on the entire family and children in particular.

The second article is entitled "Kinship Care: A Cultural Resource of African American and Latino Families Coping with Parental Substance Abuse." This article provides an in-depth discussion of kinship support within a cultural context for African American and Latino families. The article presents a culturally focussed conceptual model of treatment that individuals and agencies could use in providing substance abuse services to African American and Latino families.

The third article is entitled "The Role of Hawaiian Elders in Substance Abuse Treatment Among Asian/Pacific Islander Women." This article presents the results of a study that examined the benefits of involving Hawaiian elders in the substance abuse treatment of women of Asian/Pacific Islander background. This article is also unique because it discusses an ancient native Hawaiian family intervention strategy called "Ho'oponopono."

The fourth article is entitled "Perceptions of Parental Support by HIV Positive Asian and Pacific Islander American Gay Sons." This article presents the results of a study that investigated the extent and types of social support Asian and Pacific Islander homosexual males received from their parents when they shared with them that they were

[Haworth co-indexing entry note]: "Introduction." Delva, Jorge. Co-published simultaneously in *Journal of Family Social Work* (The Haworth Press, Inc.) Vol. 4, No. 4, 2000, pp. 1-2; and: *Substance Abuse Issues Among Families in Diverse Populations* (ed: Jorge Delva) The Haworth Press, Inc., 2000, pp. 1-2. Single or multiple copies of this article are available for a fee from The Haworth Document Delivery Service [1-800-342-9678, 9:00 a.m. - 5:00 p.m. (EST). E-mail address: getinfo@haworthpressinc.com].

gay and that they were HIV positive. This is the first study to document in the Asian/Pacific male population the process of disclosure about being gay to their parents and their parental responses. Both personal and cultural factors affecting the disclosure and responses are presented.

The fifth article is entitled "Perspectives on Family Substance Abuse: The Voices of Long-Term Al-Anon Members." This article presents the results of interviews conducted with Al-Anon members about their experiences in seeing their spouses slowly slip into alcoholism. It documents the difficulties and the hopes of the spouses living in a relationship with someone who has an alcohol problem. The article also describes the way these individuals have benefited from participating in the self-help program of Al-Anon.

The sixth and final article is entitled "Effects of Family Involvement on Length of Stay and Treatment Completion Rates with Cocaine and Alcohol Abusers." This article is an important contribution to the substance abuse field as it tested the effectiveness of substance abuse treatment programs. Specifically, this article presents the findings of a study designed to test the effects of family participation in the treatment of individuals with cocaine and alcohol problems. Findings from this study provide evidence that family involvement increased the likelihood that people with alcohol and cocaine problems would complete the full course of treatment.

Jorge Delva, PhD

Conditional Welfare:
A Family Social Work Perspective
on Mandatory Drug Testing

Michael S. Spencer, PhD
Jordana R. Muroff, MSW
Jorge Delva, PhD

SUMMARY. Drug testing of welfare applicants as a requirement for benefits, its pros and cons, and its implications for family social work practice are discussed in this paper. While proponents of drug testing argue that drug use and welfare dependency are correlated, opponents suggest that mandatory drug testing is costly, infringes upon individuals' civil rights, and unfairly assumes welfare applicants are drug abusers. Client and family concerns around mandatory drug testing and positive test results include the possibility of child welfare system involvement, reduced employment opportunities, and the lack of adequate child care while in treatment. Effective treatment models for substance abusing welfare applicants and recipients should occur within a system of collabora-

Michael S. Spencer is Assistant Professor, School of Social Work, and Faculty Associate, Center on Poverty, Risk, and Mental Health, University of Michigan, Ann Arbor, MI. Jordana R. Muroff is a joint PhD student in Social Work and Psychology, University of Michigan, Arbor, MI. Jorge Delva is Assistant Professor, School of Social Work, Florida State University, Tallahassee, FL.

Address correspondence to: Dr. Michael S. Spencer, Assistant Professor, School of Social Work, and Faculty Associate, Center on Poverty, Risk, and Mental Health, University of Michigan, 540 East Liberty, Suite 202, Ann Arbor, MI 48104-2210.

The authors wish to thank Jennifer Jolley and Terri Torkko for their assistance.

The preparation of this manuscript was supported by the National Institute of Mental Health (NIMH) Social Work Research Development Center on Poverty, Risk, and Mental Health at the University of Michigan (MH 51363).

[Haworth co-indexing entry note]: "Conditional Welfare: A Family Social Work Perspective on Mandatory Drug Testing." Spencer, Michael S., Jordana R. Muroff, and Jorge Delva. Co-published simultaneously in *Journal of Family Social Work* (The Haworth Press, Inc.) Vol. 4, No. 4, 2000, pp. 3-14; and: *Substance Abuse Issues Among Families in Diverse Populations* (ed: Jorge Delva) The Haworth Press, Inc., 2000, pp. 3-14. Single or multiple copies of this article are available for a fee from The Haworth Document Delivery Service [1-800-342-9678, 9:00 a.m. - 5:00 p.m. (EST). E-mail address: getinfo@haworthpressinc.com].

3

tive care that includes the entire family, particularly the children of these substance-abusing parents. Training issues for family social work practitioners and social work educators are also discussed. *[Article copies available for a fee from The Haworth Document Delivery Service: 1-800-342-9678. E-mail address: <getinfo@haworthpressinc.com> Website: <http://www.haworth pressinc.com>]*

KEYWORDS. Substance abuse, welfare, drug-testing, poverty, policy

INTRODUCTION

This paper provides an overview of recent legislation mandating drug testing for welfare recipients and a discussion of its implications for family social work practice. We examine practice and treatment issues for individuals who may test positive for drugs under the new law, as well as training issues for social work educators and professionals. We conclude with recommendations for effective models of practice that may be useful in the treatment of low-income individuals with substance abuse problems.

BACKGROUND

On the heels of President Clinton's proclamation to "end welfare as we know it," the U.S. Congress enacted the 1996 Personal Responsibility and Work Opportunity Reconciliation Act (PRWORA). As the centerpiece of this country's welfare reform, PRWORA ended Aid to Families with Dependent Children (AFDC) and replaced it with Temporary Assistance for Needy Families (TANF). TANF places a five-year lifetime limit on the receipt of welfare benefits and requires most welfare mothers to work no later than two years after entering the program. The motivation for the recent legislation on drug testing welfare recipients can be traced to a suspected association between drug use and welfare participation. For example, Delva and colleagues (in press) found the occurrence of any illicit drug use among welfare recipients to be 50% higher than among non-welfare recipients. Kaestner (1998) found that past-year drug use is positively related to future welfare participation, but the magnitude of the effect was only modest.

Both drug use and welfare have been noted as deterrents to work and underlying reasons for individual failure and personal irresponsibility. However, others contend that this law unfairly singles out poor individuals and that evidence of a causal relationship between drug use and welfare participation is weak. This claim is supported by data from the National Longitudinal Survey on Youth that suggests if drug use among welfare participants were reduced to the levels of non-participants, welfare participation would only decline by 3 to 5% (Kaestner, 1998).

Proponents of the law indicate that substance abuse not only affects the abuser, but also the abuser's family, community, and other state programs such as the Children's Protective Services (CPS) and the justice system. Therefore, the goal of the law is to help welfare applicants become independent of drugs and welfare, break down the barriers to employment, and reduce the risks to children of substance abusers. Perhaps the most influential argument for testing welfare applicants for drug use has to do with strong negative attitudes towards drug use and the belief that it contributes to the breakdown of the moral fabric of society–that drug use is intolerable and a sign of a character deficit, the same kind of character deficit that is said to be the underlying cause of urban poverty and welfare dependency.

Opponents of mandatory drug testing feel that the law is fraught with problems and that there are many unanswered questions. From an economic standpoint, opponents point to the costs of a drug-testing program. In fact, cost was an important reason drug-testing programs were not implemented in several states, including Louisiana, New York, and Maryland. Testimony submitted to the House Committee on Family and Children Services suggests that there should be a focus on identifying and treating recipients who have shown an inability to hold jobs because of substance abuse rather than spend millions of dollars testing everyone.

Others argue that the high costs of drug testing will divert money from other programs that might be used to treat substance abuse and other mental health problems. A study of barriers to employment among female welfare recipients in Michigan (Danziger et al., 1999) found that mental health problems occur at much higher rates compared to women in national samples. Substantial percentages of respondents indicated that they had not completed high school, possessed few skills, reported multiple incidences of perceived workplace discrimination, and lacked access to a car or had no driver's license. Danziger and colleagues (1999) also reported that multiple barriers were more common than single barriers among this welfare sample, where almost two-thirds experienced two or more barriers to work and over a quarter had four or more. Interestingly, welfare mothers were found no more likely to be drug and alcohol dependent than a general sample of women.

Another argument used by opponents of drug testing is that it unfairly equates being poor with substance abuse. The American Civil Liberties Union states that individuals should not have to relinquish their Fourth Amendment right to privacy because they have to ask the government for help. The U.S. Constitution guarantees that no individual can be subjected to a search by the government unless there is a reasonable suspicion that they have committed some crime or based on probable cause that a law has been violated. Thus, mandatory drug testing assumes that welfare applicants are substance abusers and that being poor is a crime. Poor mothers who seek welfare assistance often have little to no options available, making them very vulnerable and in no position to offer opposition to drug testing requirements. If consent for testing were obtained, it is questionable as to whether it would be considered voluntary.

Drug testing also raises issues related to treatment for substance abuse. While states are anticipating short-term outpatient treatment options, long-term residential treatment may be necessary. However, residential treatment facilities may not be able to accommodate children, and women may be less likely to enter residential treatment if adequate child care is not available or if doing so means giving up their children to foster care (Strawn, 1997). Funding for residential treatment may also be problematic as Medicaid regulations prohibit spending on services to individuals in an institution of mental disease with more than 16 beds. Thus, many states limit inpatient substance abuse treatment services to short-term detoxification and hospital emergency services.

Finally, and perhaps most distressing, is the potential consequences for welfare-eligible families who choose not to apply for benefits because of mandatory drug testing. Applying for welfare is a humbling and potentially humiliating experience. Requiring drug tests adds to this negative experience–enough so that it may be a powerful deterrent to applying for benefits. It is unclear at this point if people will be willing to submit to testing and treatment in order to receive benefits or not. Rather than helping families, the new law may have the negative consequence of pushing women with serious substance abuse problems further away from help.

FAMILY SOCIAL WORK PERSPECTIVE

It is critical that family social workers be well-versed in welfare reform and understand and respond to clients' ensuing concerns. Family social workers must be well-trained in developing and executing appropriate family treatment plans, as well as reaching out to those in need who do not apply for benefits because of mandated drug testing. Specifically, family social workers must be able to address client concerns around the following issues: (1) the child welfare system's involvement and the fear of losing their children, (2) the stigma of testing positive, (3) securing employment, and (4) the availability of child care while at work and/or in drug treatment.

Parents who test positive for drugs, or are concerned that they might test positive, may fear that such results will lead to their children's placement in foster care. Applicants may distrust the child welfare system and fear that a positive test will be used as evidence of incompetence or neglectful parenting. While some view drug-dependent mothers as incurious regarding their children's needs and remorseless in prioritizing drugs over their children, many of these mothers value their roles as parents and note the stability that their children bring to their lives. Most drug-abusing mothers express great shame and guilt regarding their neglect of their children (Colten, 1982; Kearney, Murphy, & Rosenbaum, 1994; Luthar & Walsh, 1995). Furthermore, a pregnant woman may fear that a positive drug test could lead to the loss of her maternal rights to her unborn child and/or criminal prosecution. Similar fears may also deter mothers from receiving prenatal care (Colby & Murrell, 1998).

Family social workers must be sensitive to how positive test results affect both the individual and family. Some individuals who test positive for drugs may have an extreme addiction, while others may be occasional users whose use has had little or no destructive impact on their lives or their families. While depression, anxiety, antisocial attitudes, and deficits in cognitive functioning, among other problems, may be co-morbid with drug use, other psychopathology may have been hidden by or attributed to the substance abuse (Eliason & Skinstad, 1995). Despite the desire to quit, some individuals may rely on drugs as a coping mechanism and source of support, and therefore fear facing life drug-free (Akin & Gregoire, 1997).

While welfare recipients are entitled to cash and health benefits, clients (or potential clients) who are mandated to undergo drug treatment may be concerned with adhering to the deadlines for securing employment and maintaining time-limited benefits. The time period imposed by TANF, requiring welfare recipients to secure employment within two years, and the five-year limit on benefits may be partly or entirely consumed by mandated drug treatment. Therefore, it may not be possible or realistic to expect welfare applicants who test positive for drug use and are mandated to treatment to meet the employment requirements within the time parameters. Welfare recipients need to be informed of the expectations and time-limitations as dictated by the policy and be linked to resources (such as drug treatment, job training, benefit providers, etc.) in order to fulfill these requirements. Stigma may affect securing employment, for if positive drug test results are communicated to potential employers, this may reduce job prospects or affect the employers' and fellow employees' perceptions. This raises further questions as to how social workers or policy makers will link communities and companies and encourage businesses to hire individuals in recovery. Complications in employment due to relapse need consideration as well. It is critical that family social workers are up-to-date regarding benefits, resources, and available training programs to which their clients are entitled.

Even after obtaining employment, clients may be concerned with the lack of available and affordable child-care options in low-income communities. These mothers may need to rely more heavily on family and friends who are already taxed, other informal arrangements, or leave their children unsupervised, all of which may be inadequate or potentially dangerous. Women who test positive for drug use and require residential treatment may be concerned about the lack of available child-care options while in treatment.

CLINICAL TRAINING ISSUES

To some, the welfare system has been deemed uncaring, unsupportive, and overburdened. Akin and Gregoire's study (1997) of parents who have recovered from addiction and have been involved with the child welfare system indicates that clients with drug use problems believed their social workers did not understand the impact addiction has on individuals and families. The authors recant the stories of social workers' reneged promises, inattention, apathy, and disrespect, unrealistic expectations on the part of the agency, and a lack of strength-based, client-focused approaches. However, examples of positive relationships between clients and social workers based on honesty, sincerity, and careful listening also are reported.

Research indicates that social workers have not received adequate training for addiction problems (Gregoire, 1994; Kagle, 1987; King & Lorenson, 1989; Morehouse, 1978; Peyton, 1980; Thompson, 1990). According to a study by Van Wormer (1987), helping professionals traditionally ignore problems associated with alcoholism. Kagle (1987) reported that in 83% of cases she examined, social workers did not record or address a client's alcohol problem.

Several researchers have identified factors that contribute to effective practice (Akin & Gregoire, 1997; Tracy & Farkas, 1994). The worker-client relationship is valued by clients when the worker is honest, resourceful, considers the clients' perspective, hopeful and non-judgmental, shares power, provides choices, assists in realistic goal-setting, believes in their client, empowers clients, and views them as a person versus a case. Welfare practitioners need more knowledge of treatment systems for drug and alcohol abuse, symptoms of alcohol or drug-related addictions, the dynamics of families with a substance-abusing parent, and intergenerational patterns of drug or alcohol abuse (McMahon & Luthar, 1998). Furthermore, family social workers must be informed of the welfare and child welfare systems' policies and procedures and networks for parent support. Knowledge of the effects of parent-child separation and skills to identify signs of child abuse and neglect are also critical to effective practice. Social workers working with substance-abusing parents need specialized skills in interviewing, engagement, assessment, goal-setting, intervention, termination of services, and evaluation. Training in aggressive case management, relapse prevention, and family preservation techniques is critical in order to fulfill the multiple needs and goals of families (Tracy & Farkas, 1994).

It is crucial that social work training programs acknowledge and educate their students about various family systems, including traditional, blended, single parent, cohabiting, intergenerational, same-sex, homeless, foster parent, and matched families (Freeman, 1993) and be sensitive and respectful to the client's own definition and perceptions regarding family. Social workers need to be trained to use intervention techniques that are sensitive to the influences of culture and socio-economic status. Due to the diverse needs of those who use substances, adequate training must incorporate more integrative or collaborative approaches to practice and treatment.

TREATMENT INTERVENTIONS

There are various drug and alcohol treatment interventions. They include detoxification, outpatient treatment programs, intensive outpatient programs, inpatient or residential treatment programs, therapeutic communities and halfway houses, and self-help groups (Feig, 1998; Marion & Coleman, 1991). Through detoxification, an individual safely withdraws from alcohol or drugs while under medical supervision. It is a short-term program and is an initial step toward becoming substance-free. Outpatient treatment programs provide individual and/or group services, such as counseling and education regarding addiction and recovery, for a few hours per week. Meanwhile, inpatient or residential treatment programs are 24-hour facilities, located in hospitals or non-medical rehabilitation settings geared toward individuals with more severe addictions to substances. Length of service ranges from a few weeks to several months. Long-term living situations structured for supporting recovering individuals as they transition back into the community are referred to as therapeutic communities or halfway houses. Substance users may also come together and form self-help groups that help members recognize the effects of drugs and/or alcohol on their lives and utilize a step-approach toward recovery. Self-help groups such as Alcoholics Anonymous and Narcotics Anonymous are informal and do not include professional involvement (Feig, 1998).

COLLABORATIVE CARE

Drug use has major implications for the entire family; however, drug treatment programs generally do not assess families and children or consider issues such as ties with a spouse or partner, the parent-child relationship, and the stage of development of children as a critical part of treatment (McMahon & Luthar, 1998). Public welfare agencies, child welfare systems, school systems, child-guidance clinics, and substance abuse treatment systems are separate systems structured in a manner that complicates interagency collaboration.

McMahon and Luthar (1998) address conflicts that develop between these various agencies. One source of conflict may be differences in philosophy regarding the nature of the drug use problem. Substance abuse may be considered a health problem, a social problem, or a criminal problem. Agencies have varying agendas and multiple perspectives on resolving challenges and establishing and reaching goals. The child's need for permanence may conflict with the parent's need for substance treatment, while other agencies may disagree about the appropriateness of keeping the family unit intact. Clients may face conflicting and inflexible service policies and procedures of multiple systems. Collaboration between agencies may require more time and is not financially profitable. Each agency has its own culture that may influence the professional values, stereotypes, prejudices, and misconceptions of other agencies or the clients they serve. A history of problematic relations may also compromise the development of collaborative efforts.

EFFECTIVE MODELS OF FAMILY PRACTICE

The literature includes various treatment models and approaches for families affected by drug use. According to McMahon and Luthar (1998), there are many critical considerations in developing family-oriented approaches to interventions including: (1) cultural context, (2) the treatment setting [level of care, philosophical orientation of the program], (3) the age of the children, (4) gender of abuser, (5) the primary drug abused, (6) resolution of questions of ethics, values, and laws, (7) demonstrating efficacy [by saving money and preserving the family], and (8) securing financial support. Securing financial support is complex due to the pressures to contain costs and limit treatment to short-term care despite the need for long-term preventive services that may defer cost-savings. Legislators and administrators struggle to determine the most effective approach to funding, given that a single sum of money is allocated, yet each family is served by numerous systems (McMahon & Luthar, 1998).

A family approach to treatment also should include the children of the substance-abusing parent. For example, a group work model for treatment with children from chemically dependent families may include education regarding addiction, reflection, and sharing of personal experiences and feelings (McRoy, Aguilar, & Shorkey, 1993). Wegscheider (1981) proposes a treatment model that includes the whole family system. Under this model, the substance-dependent family member receives primary treatment while all family members undergo a separate, simultaneous treatment during the first 4-6 weeks of substance-abuse treatment. The following 10-12 weeks involve individual therapy and/or multifamily therapy. Practitioners should also be aware of the problems that may interrupt treatment, including funding shortages impacting treatment availability for family members, family members' refusal of treatment, divorce, or the placement of children in foster care or the homes of relatives (McRoy, Aguilar, & Shorkey, 1993).

NEEDS AND CHALLENGES

More information about the issues and concerns of mandating drug testing for welfare recipients is needed. An important challenge to the implementation of drug testing programs concerns the types of services offered to individuals with substance abuse problems. If treatment is an important goal of the program, state officials must assure that there are adequate and effective models of treatment in place. Specifically, adequate facilities will be necessary to meet the needs of long-term residential treatment, as well as adequate funding for these treatment programs. In addition to treatment, there must be sufficient funding for after-care programs that maintain abstinence over time.

There must also be greater effort toward maintaining collaborative relationships between the different systems that might serve individuals with substance abuse problems, including public welfare agencies, child welfare systems, school systems, justice systems, child development specialists, and health care providers. Collaboration between these systems could lead to the identification of women who do not seek out welfare benefits but are in need of assistance with their drug problems. Substance abuse treatment programs must expand their efforts to work not only with the substance-abusing parents, but also their children. Alternative programs that provide for child-care supports while parents are recovering should be developed. These programs might include parenting programs and interventions to help parents understand the consequences of their drug use on their children and their healthy development. The well-being of the children in these poor families must become the priority. Currently, laws that mandate drug testing show little regard for the welfare of children. Rather, these laws focus on punitive measures and sanctions for women who do not comply with treatment. Unfortunately, the well-being of children has been an afterthought in much of the welfare reform legislation to date. Thus, a major challenge to social workers and social work researchers will be the continued advocacy of children and children's rights under these new laws. Further research that examines the relationship between the provisions of these new laws and children's well-being is also needed.

REFERENCES

Akin, B.A., & Gregoire, T.K. (1997). Parents' views on child welfare's response to addiction. Families in Society: *The Journal of Contemporary Human Services 78*, 393-404.

Colten, M.E. (1982). Attitudes, experiences, and self-perceptions of heroin-addicted mothers. *Journal of Social Issues 38*, 77-92.

Colby, S.M., & Murrell, W. (1998) Child welfare and substance abuse services: From barriers to collaboration. In R.L. Hampton, V. Senatore, and T.P. Gullotta (Eds.), *Substance Abuse, Family Violence, and Child Welfare: Bridging Perspectives* (pp. 188-219). Thousand Oaks, CA: Sage Publications, Inc.

Danziger, S.K., Corcoran, M., Danziger, S., Heflin, C., Kalil, A., Levine, J., Rosen, D., Seefeldt, K., Siefert, K., & Tolman, R. (1999, April). *Barriers to the employment of welfare recipients*. Poverty Research and Training Center, University of Michigan. Retrieved October 21, 1999, from the World Wide Web: <http://www.ssw.umich.edu/poverty/wesappam.pdf>.

Delva, J., Neumark, Y.D., Furr, C.D.M., & Anthony, J.A. (in press). Drug use among welfare recipients in the United States. *The American Journal of Alcohol and Drug Abuse*.

Eliason, M.L., & Skinstad, A.H. (1995). Drug/alcohol addictions and mothering. *Alcohol Treatment Quarterly, 12*, 83-96.

Feig, L. (1998) Understanding the problem: The gap between substance abuse programs and welfare services. In R.L. Hampton, V. Senatore, and T.P. Gullotta (Eds.), *Substance Abuse, Family Violence, and Child Welfare: Bridging Perspectives* (pp. 62-95). Thousand Oaks, CA: Sage Publications, Inc.

Freeman, E.M. (1993). *Substance Abuse Treatment: A Family Perspective*. Newbury Park, CA: Sage Publications, Inc.

Gregoire, T.K. (1994). Assessing the benefits and increasing the utility of addiction training for public child welfare workers: A pilot study. *Child Welfare 73*, 69-81.

Kaestner, R. (1998). Drug use and AFDC participation: Is there a connection? *Journal of Policy Analysis and Management 17*, 495-520.

Kagle, J. (1987). Secondary prevention of substance abuse. *Social Work 32*, 446-448.

Kearney, M.H., Murphy, S., & Rosenbaum, M. (1994). Mothering on crack: A grounded theory analysis. *Social Science and Medicine 38*, 351-361.

King, G., & Lorenson, J. (1989). Alcoholism training for social workers, *Social Casework 70*, 375-382.

Luthar, S.S., & Walsh, K.G. (1995). Treatment needs of drug addicted mothers: Integrated parenting psychotherapy interventions. *Journal of Substance Abuse Treatment 12*, 341-348.

Marion, T.R., & Coleman, K. (1991). Recovery issues and treatment resources. In D.C. Daley (Ed.). *Treating the Chemically Dependent and Their Families* (pp. 100-127). Newbury Park, CA: Sage Publications, Inc.

McMahon, T.J., & Luthar, S.S. (1998). Bridging the gap for children as their parents enter substance abuse treatment. In R.L. Hampton, V. Senatore, & T.P. Gullotta (Eds.). *Substance Abuse, Family Violence, and Child Welfare: Bridging Perspectives* (pp. 143-187). Thousand Oaks, CA: Sage Publications, Inc.

McRoy, R.G., Aguilar, M.A., & Shorkey, C.T. (1993). A cross-cultural treatment approach for families with young children. In E.M. Freeman (Ed.). *Substance Abuse Treatment: A Family Perspective* (pp. 23-47). Newbury Park, CA: Sage Publications, Inc.

Morehouse, E.R. (1978). Treating the alcoholic on public assistance. *Social Casework 59*, 36-41.

Peyton, S. (1980). Willingness to treat alcoholics: A study of graduate social work students. *Journal of Studies on Alcohol 41*, 935-940.

Strawn, J. (1997, January 7). Issue notes: Substance abuse and welfare reform policy [online resource]. Retrieved October 17, 1999 from the World Wide Web: <http://www.welfareinfo.org/hardtoplace.htm>.

Thompson, L. (1990). Working with alcoholic families in a child welfare agency: The problem of underdiagnosis. *Child Welfare 69*, 464-470.

Tracy, E.M., & Farkas, K.J. (1994). Preparing practitioners for child welfare with substance-abusing families, *Child Welfare 73*, 57-68.

Van Wormer, K. (1987). Training social work students for practice with substance abusers: An ecological approach. *Journal of Social Work Education 23*, 47-56.

Wegscheider, S. (1981). *Another Chance: Hope and Health for the Alcoholic Family.* Palo Alto, CA: Science and Behavior Books.

Kinship Care:
A Cultural Resource
of African American and Latino Families
Coping with Parental Substance Abuse

Concepcion Barrio, PhD
Margaret J. Hughes, PhD

SUMMARY. This paper examines kinship care as a cultural resource used by African American and Latino families coping with substance abuse by a family member. Although there is a growing body of literature on kinship care, there are no conceptual or empirical studies that have drawn or built on cultural similarities between these two groups of ethnic minority families. A framework that prioritizes cultural assessment and relevance in using familial and cultural resources is proposed to assist practitioners confronted with the demographic realities of working with social, clinical and ethnocultural complexities when serving ethnic minority families. The framework is based on practice implications raised by recent studies on kinship care and from the perspective of pertinent cross-cultural and anthropological literature. *[Article copies available for a fee from The Haworth Document Delivery Service: 1-800-342-9678. E-mail address: <getinfo@haworthpressinc.com> Website: <http://www.haworthpressinc.com>]*

KEYWORDS. Kinship care, African American families, Latino families, cultural resources, cultural assessment

Concepcion Barrio and Margaret J. Hughes are Assistant Professors, School of Social Work, San Diego State University, 5500 Campanile Drive, San Diego, CA 92139.

[Haworth co-indexing entry note]: "Kinship Care: A Cultural Resource of African American and Latino Families Coping with Parental Substance Abuse." Barrio, Concepcion, and Margaret J. Hughes. Co-published simultaneously in *Journal of Family Social Work* (The Haworth Press, Inc.) Vol. 4, No. 4, 2000, pp. 15-31; and: *Substance Abuse Issues Among Families in Diverse Populations* (ed: Jorge Delva) The Haworth Press, Inc., 2000, pp. 15-31. Single or multiple copies of this article are available for a fee from The Haworth Document Delivery Service [1-800-342-9678, 9:00 a.m. - 5:00 p.m. (EST). E-mail address: getinfo@haworthpress inc.com].

15

INTRODUCTION

Recent literature on ethnic minority families has begun to recognize cultural resources and resilience of African American and Latino[1] families in coping with health and mental health problems affecting the family system (Parra & Guarnaccia, 1998; Stevenson & Renard, 1993; Taylor, 1994a). Ethnic minority cultures are typically centered on the family and supported by extended kin and formal and informal community networks (Lefley, 1990). These cultures generally emerge from collectivistic, sociocentric societies. Among African American and Latino households, the web of relationships that extends across close and distant relatives and nonrelatives and across generations provides a support network that is sustained by affiliative emotional traditions and rules of mutual obligation (Moore-Hines, Garcia-Preto, McGoldrick, Almeida, & Weltman, 1999). An extended family and multigenerational structure, undergirded by sociocentric cultural values and traditions, creates conditions for the care and support of family members in times of need. In the child welfare field, this caregiving system of support, nurturance and protection provided by relatives and fictive kin to children who must be separated from their parents is known as kinship care (Wilhelmus, 1998).

The focus of this paper is on African American and Latino families because of their high rates of kinship care placements. Although kinship care has a long tradition in these cultures, and a large number of kinship caregivers exists within informal and extended family networks (Fuller-Thomson, Minkler & Driver, 1997; McLean & Thomas, 1996), much of the literature is limited to formal kinship care placements within the purview of the child welfare system. A comprehensive discussion of the parental and children's issues that intersect with kinship care is beyond the scope of this article. The purpose is to examine kinship care as a cultural resource among these two groups of ethnic families dealing with substance abuse by a family member. Conceptual and empirical studies that build on the cultural commonalities of these two groups of ethnic minority families are lacking in the literature on kinship care. A framework that prioritizes cultural assessment and relevance in using familial and cultural resources is proposed to assist practitioners confronted with the demographic realities and the attendant clinical and sociocultural complexities in working with ethnic minority families. The framework is based on practice implications raised by recent studies on kinship care and from the perspective of pertinent cross-cultural and anthropological literature.

THE PROBLEM

Illicit substance use is one of the most critical social problems in the United States. The 1996 National Household Survey on Drug Abuse reported over 13 million illicit drug users. Crack cocaine was the most widely used drug; however, heroin use rose 217% from 1993 to 1996 (National Institute on Drug Abuse, 1999). Drug abuse can negatively affect all aspects of a person's life including health, employment, education and relationships. It is particularly devastating to family stability and, along with other social factors (divorce, teenage pregnancy, child abuse and abandonment) and health factors such as HIV/ AIDS, has significantly contributed to the separation of parents from their children (Berrick, Barth, & Needell, 1994; Burton, 1992; Hayslip, Shore, Henderson, & Lambert, 1998). Additionally, substance abuse problems are frequently accompanied by psychiatric comorbidity that can overwhelm and debilitate families with such risks and conditions as depression, suicidality, psychosis, and homelessness (Maser, Cassano, & Michelini, 1997).

Problems stemming from parental substance abuse are estimated to account for 50% to 80% of cases of child maltreatment in the child welfare system and the dramatic increase in kinship care placements (Pruchno, 1999; Morrison-Dore & Doris, 1998). Over half a million children were in foster care in 1996 (O'Laughlin, 1998). Some estimates indicate this number is nearly a one hundred percent increase from the mid-1980s. Recent changes in law under the Adoption and Safe Families Act of 1997 were prompted by the continuing *drift* of children from one foster care placement to another with an estimated 15,000 aging out of the system (du Pont, 1997, Oct. 29). It is therefore not surprising that in the past decade, kinship foster care was found to be the fastest growing funded service within the child welfare system in response needs of an increasing number of children affected by parental use of crack cocaine, particularly in inner cities and economically disadvantaged communities (Morrison-Dore & Doris, 1998; Scannapieco & Hegar, 1999).

In 1993, seven percent of African American and four percent of Latino children were in out-of-home care as compared to three percent of all children (U.S. Bureau of the Census, 1994). Reports indicate that although all ethnic, racial and economic groups are represented in kinship families, most children served in these placements are disproportionately African Americans and Latinos (Scannapieco & Hegar, 1999). African Americans in some urban cities comprise as high as 90% of kinship foster care placements (Dubowitz, Tepper, Feigelman, Sawyer, & Davidson, 1990). Although, there are fewer studies on Latinos, Burnette (1999a) argues that because of the high concentration of Latino groups in large urban centers and their concomitant socioeconomic problems, the rate of skipped-generation Latino households may be similar to that of African Americans. Grandparents head the majority of kinship care placements also known as skipped-generation households (Burnette, 1999a). Several studies confirm that parental substance abuse was the primary reason for grandparents raising their grandchildren (Besharov, 1989; Burton, 1992). Forty-four percent of more than 1000 grandparents surveyed in a study conducted by the American Association of Retired Persons in Washington, D.C. cited parental drug problems as the reason for taking their grandchildren into their homes (Hall, 1998). Almost half of the children in kinship placements have a history of exposure to drugs or alcohol (Nisivoccia, 1996). Substance abuse also has emerged as a significant reason for the continuation of kinship care. In a study by Gleeson, O'Donnel and Bonecutter (1997), 81% of 77 participating families cited substance abuse as the primary problem preventing the return of their grandchildren to their biological parents.

BENEFITS AND STRENGTHS OF KINSHIP CARE

The cultural tradition of kinship care among African American and Latino families is being formally tapped as a natural resource for bridging the care of children and preserving families (Burnette, 1999ab). The benefits of kinship care are straightforward and vitally important: the support and protection of children and the maintenance of meaningful emotional ties and family connections while planning for permanence (Nisivoccia, 1996). Kinship care has an established tradition as a means of preserving the ethnic minority family and, with an increase in need for out-of-home placements and a decrease in formal foster care homes, has become a viable source for the child welfare system (Children's Defense Fund, 1994). These cultural practices contribute greatly to the positive development of troubled children and preservation of family systems (Danzy & Jackson, 1997). Studies have shown that children removed from their birth parents and initially placed in kinship care arrangements overcome many of the negative side effects of nonrelative, traditional foster care placements and experience a more stable development (Scannapieco, Hegar, & McAlpine, 1997; Usher, Randolph, & Gogan, 1999). Children experience more stability as they are likely to remain in one home rather than multiple placements, which characterize the traditional foster care system, and are at less risk of maltreatment than children placed in homes outside the family (Nisivoccia, 1996).

Older adult relatives are special resources for children to learn cultural traditions, acquire strong cultural values, and experience positive memories and identities of their biological parents. These benefits may otherwise be lost to the children's painful experiences that led to their out-of-home placement. The significant role of grandparents as cultural custodians for ethnic minorities (Smith-Barusch & Steen, 1996) offers children not only emotional continuity but also an essential biological family continuity for the development of ethnic identity.

The strengths and benefits of kinship care have received recognition from professional and academic groups and organizations. Kinship care was specifically cited as part of the service continuum in federal guidelines for the Family Preservation and Support Services Act of 1993. Black Administrators in Child Welfare advocates that African American child welfare scholars and social workers view kinship care as a component of family preservation services (Danzy & Jackson, 1997). The importance of providing ethnic minority children with familial continuity and a sense of belonging is emphasized as the direct benefit of kinship care. Family and cultural preservation are congruent with the concept of kinship care, particularly for the African American community and its sociocentric orientation (Danzy & Jackson, 1997).

AFRICAN AMERICAN FAMILIES

Cultural groups of African decent in the United States show diversity in community and family practices. However, the support system of kinship or extended family, including adult relatives and fictive kin, remains a common characteristic (Everett, Chipungu, & Leashore, 1991). A broad definition of family, incorporating an informal network of kin and community, is tied to the legacy of slavery, African traditions and worldviews characterized by collectivism, spiritualism and interdependence (Baldwin & Hopkins, 1990; Moore Hines, 1999). Based on this heritage, it is not surprising that evidence of surrogate parenting by grandparents and other relatives exists before the Civil War era and up to current times (Burton, 1992; Hill, 1971).

Africentric family tradition places responsibility for raising children on both the nuclear and extended families (Billingsley, 1992; Carter, 1997; Stack, 1974). Family theorists have recognized the rich cultural traditions that have sustained African American families across generations and through pervasive and adverse social conditions (Moore-Hines, 1999). The Africentric principles of connectedness, caring, and mutual aid, among others (Moore-Hines) are actualized in familial support, networks and kinship care together with the sustaining source of support from the church in family and community life (Carter, 1997; Lefley, 1990). Moore-Hines refers to the African proverb, "If I don't care for you, I don't care for myself," as a cultural reflection of the interdependence and caring that depicts the source of cultural strengths and characterizes the collective responsibility of the family system.

Although African American families like other ethnic minority and nonminority families evidence heterogeneous family structures, in general they are characterized as matrifocal (Burnette, 1999b; Taylor, 1994b). However, insofar as the roles and patterns of authority, African American families exhibit an egalitarianism, meaning complementarity and flexibility in familial and gender roles among adult members (Taylor, 1994b). The role of elders is revered as grandparents take on an active part of the extended network providing custodial care for young children and offer support to adults going through both positive and difficult life transitions (Carter, 1997). African American grandmothers are likely to have peers who also live with their grandchildren and to come from multigenerational backgrounds (Pruchno, 1999).

LATINO FAMILIES

In acknowledging the great diversity among Latino groups in the United States, it is also important to emphasize that this diversity is reflected in variations in family patterns and traditions. Differences based on country of origin, social class and economic status, immigration history, and level of acculturation are among some of the salient factors that should be recognized for their potential influence on family practices. For the purpose of this discussion several general characteristics relevant to cultural traditions of kinship care will be highlighted. Several Latino groups, particularly those originating from North and Central American countries, share a legacy of colonization of their indigenous ancestors, the continuing and residual effects of which are associated with the structural inequalities and ethnic and socioeconomic oppression experienced in their countries of origin and in the United States (Baca Zinn, 1994). As with African Americans, an indigenous heritage also represents a source of rich cultural tradition thought to influence sense of self, worldviews, spiritualism and familism. Falicov (1998) refers to the familial self or *familismo* as the common thread shared by many Latino groups. Religious rituals are cultural and social events that often correspond with developmental and life cycle transitions and involve expectations of behavior in supporting familial and community cultural traditions (Falicov, 1999).

Although, many variations exist in the types of family structure among Latino families, patriarchal families and extensive kinship systems generally characterize Latino groups. Typically men occupy an active role in household affairs, and women take on an active role in caregiving and decision-making that, with age, affords them prestige and authority within the family (Burnette, 1999b). Among Puerto Rican and Mexican-heritage people, the extensive kinship and co-parenting system, founded on formal and informal god-parenting relationships, is known as *compadrazgo*. The compadrazgo tradition amplifies the extended family network with fictive kin who sponsor a child or adult in one of the religious occasions of baptism, first communion, confirmation or marriage (Baca Zinn, 1994; Carrasquillo, 1994; Falicov, 1999). Involvement in this tradition brings both honor and responsibility, entailing a life-long commitment in family life through material and emotional gift giving.

In some families, extended members, particularly elders or fictive kin, can take the role of secondary caregiver for children or adults undergoing various life transitions or crises (Burnette, 1999b). The practice of informally adopting children as *hijos de crianza* is regarded as an expression of affection and family bonds in response to meeting the needs of the child and the family system as a whole during times of crises, family instability, or death of the biological parents (Carrasquillo, 1994). Historically, strong familism with its extended family patterns has buffered and facilitated the adaptation of people through adverse racial and economic conditions in the United States (Baca-Zinn, 1994). Reports indicate that in large cities there are comparable proportions of African American and Latino grandparents who make up skipped-generation families (Burnette, 1999a); however, Latino elders tend to live in larger households, which afford them greater family interaction and support than African American elders (Burnette, 1999b).

CULTURAL COMMONALITIES

This brief overview of African American and Latino families is not intended to dismiss the heterogeneity or the distinct cultural features of these families. However, it is notable that beyond a shared ethnic minority status, there are cultural commonalities that have relevance to kinship care. Long-standing traditions of multigenerational kinship patterns and reliance on spiritualism provided a hedge against the historical legacies of slavery and colonization. This was exemplified by a tradition of cultural buffers and sources of support to cope with the difficult realities of oppression, racism and economic deprivation that accompany ethnic minority status in the United States.

The foundation of these commonalities and their cultural precedence can be understood from the perspective of the cross-cultural and anthropological literature on the sociocentric conception of the self (Kleinman, 1988). The sociocentric conception subordinates individual interests to the good of the collective. Collectivistic cultures, also termed organic and holistic, embrace a sociocentric conception of the person in relation to society. This relationship is regulated by rules of interdependence that are context-specific and govern behavior to family, relationships, and gender roles. The role of the person is guided by a culturally patterned context-dependent orientation. In collectivistic cultures, the social order is the model of nature and interdependence. The sociocentric orientation provides people with worldviews by which to guide their lives and relationships (Shweder & Bourne, 1984).

Based on a sociocentric cultural orientation, collectivistic societies show sociocentric cultural patterns which emphasize social relations and a range of conventions, rules, and roles that sustain long-term relationships preventing social isolation. They provide a structured, stable, predictable environment that allows development and healing at the person's own pace and reintegration into society (Kleinman, 1988; Shweder & Bourne, 1984). This suggests that sociocentric cultures generate natural supports leading to better social functioning for individual members undergoing health and mental health problems (Kleinman, 1988).

Ethnographic accounts (Perelberg, 1983) have shown that the ethnic family structure can be characterized as sociocentric, with delineated role relationships and a close-knit network. Emphasis may be placed on the positional relationship between members of the family, and on social roles and rules. With respect to the substance abusing family member, the sociocentric family generally becomes involved in a search for meaning of the crisis by amplifying their network and enlisting support at the community level. From this framework, a family pattern of coping emerges and provides an explanatory model embedded in a sociocentric cultural orientation. The model guides the way a family copes with crisis and how health and mental health problems are labeled, understood and managed (Kleinman, 1988; Perelberg, 1983).

Cultural conceptions of the self have also been characterized on a continuum between familistic and individualistic. These influence relational styles and determine the setting of boundaries among family members and extended networks. Considering the diversity among ethnic minority groups in the United States, Lefley (1990) pointed out that in general they share a traditional system of values. They present with cultural strengths (e.g., interdependent, group-oriented, less individualistic) that may represent protective and buffering mechanisms to deal with various problems (Lefley, 1990). Specifically, both African American and Latino ethnic groups have been described as sharing sociocentric qualities typical of cultural values which emphasize collectivity, sharing, affiliation, interdependence, and familism (Lefley 1990; Pinderhughes 1982).

Many practice and theoretical frameworks used to train practitioners and administrators are embedded in models developed without adequate consideration to diversification among ethnic cultures. For this reason, it is important to assess the sociocentric patterns; interdependence of family connections; strength of relationships and networks; and where relationships have weakened, lack balance or harmony when working with African American and Latino cultural families (Lewis-Fernandez & Kleinman, 1994). As cultural practices are reflected over time, knowledge of cultural differences and diversity extends to an understanding of intergenerational patterns and diverse family configurations such as kinship care (Goldberg-Glen, Sands, Cole & Cristofal, 1998). Presumed cultural nuance should be approached as cultural hypotheses until more information is obtained to understand their meaning (Lopez, 1997).

PROBLEMS AND CONCERNS OF KINSHIP CARE

This cultural tradition has been passed down over many generations; however, kinship care within the formal foster care system is a relatively new response to the need for more placements. Some problems affecting the use of kinship care have been identified as originating from the child welfare system. Most kinship care placements are found in large cities within poor families that lack the necessary social services and resources to hold their families together (Karp, 1996; Minkler & Roe, 1996). In most states, kinship caregivers receive lower financial assistance than traditional foster caregivers (Karp, 1996; Minkler & Roe, 1996). According to Burton (1992), grandparents raising grandchildren due to parental drug abuse received minimal economic support from the family, and results from two separate sites confirmed that greater than 50% of grandparents raising their grandchildren were "barely getting by" (p. 746).

There are the multiple negative consequences resulting from parental substance abuse that challenge many aspects of the familial system and are compounded by inadequacies of the social service delivery system. The burdens of kinship care become even greater when children have been physically and emotionally affected by the substance abuse of their parents. Although, the child welfare system is expected to intervene and facilitate in therapeutic ways, studies have found that kinship foster caregivers, especially African Americans, are provided less extensive services and are not visited as frequently by child workers when compared to traditional foster homes (Scannapieco et al., 1997).

Kinship caregivers suffer burdens when they lovingly choose to accept the challenge of raising the children of their kin. This is especially true when the caregivers are elderly. In California, New York, and Illinois where African American children comprise the majority of out-of-home placements, grandparents make up the majority of kinship care providers. In a review of the kinship care literature, Scannapieco et al. (1997) found more than 50% of kinship caregivers were grandparents and close to a third were aunts. Another study found that 61% of caregivers were grandparents, 21% aunts and uncles, and 11% siblings or other relatives (Gleeson et al., 1997). Research confirms that grandmother-headed households have fewer helpers and are the most impoverished (Pearson, 1997).

The task of raising children at an older age can bring detrimental consequences to the physical, emotional and economic well being of these providers. In addition to the multiple losses experienced in the later part of the life cycle, elderly caregivers often experience health, economic and social isolation problems. Minkler and Roe (1996) reported that among elderly caregivers increases in physical problems such as depression, insomnia and hypertension may be associated with increased stress created by unattended burdens of the caregiving role. Kinship providers may also be caregivers for spouses, biological children, and other relatives (Burton, 1992; Gleeson et al., 1997). As such, they may also become less able to continue social activities they enjoy because of additional responsibilities (Burnette, 1999b). The problems of elderly ethnic minority caregivers are further compounded by their characteristic underutilization of formal service delivery systems, including social, health and mental health services (Burnette, 1999a).

In addition to behavioral problems related to the separation of children from their parents, children who are born drug addicted or exposed to parental drug abuse often suffer from biological impairments and concurrent behavioral problems (Burton, 1992). Given the generational distance between older adult caregivers and the affected children, an additional concern is that the developmental, emotional and educational needs of the children may not be adequately met.

Fewer kinship caregivers are willing to permanently adopt the children under their care. All kinship care providers face pressure from social services to take permanent custody of their kin children. Most states discontinue the greater financial burden of caring for out-of-home children once they are permanently adopted or placed under permanent guardianship. Kin who elect permanent custody can anticipate economic burdens as well as stress from the legal ramifications of the judicial custody process (Karp, 1996). This may lead some kinship caregivers to opt out of permanent custody arrangements. Another factor in the lower rates of kinship adoptions may be the cultural belief that through the extended family concept they are already an extended surrogate parent for the child in times of need. Kinship caregivers remain hopeful that the birth parents will resume their custodial responsibility, and in reality, because parental visiting is more frequent in kinship homes, the potential for reunification is more likely (Wilhemus, 1998). Moreover, the initiation of legal, permanent custody of a kin's child may be perceived as both hurtful to the biological parents and shameful to the extended family. These beliefs may underlie the dilemma for kinship caregivers, especially if faced with the potential loss of the child to nonrelatives.

Although many of the problems that accompany formal kinship foster care are related to the impact of parental substance abuse that overtaxes already burdened families, other concerns stem from a child welfare system that has not organized the provision of services in equitable and supportive ways. Burnette (1999a) found the lack of knowledge about the availability of social services to be the main obstacle to service utilization for skipped-generation families. Considering the extent of unmet needs of the families, the findings have implications for the coordination of a wide range of family centered services based on concerted outreach efforts (Burnette). A framework is proposed to guide the cultural assessment and relevant interventions in using familial and cultural resources when serving ethnic minority families.

SUGGESTED FRAMEWORK

1. Prior to the placement process, kinship care can be considered as a viable choice, given that the individual needs of the caregiver and the child are assessed, and that adequate supports for the family can be set in place as deemed necessary (Ingram, 1996).

2. Assessment needs to include the extended family network, formal and informal natural supports, the family's history with multigenerational family living and caregiving, generational strengths, and sociocentric patterns of interdependence in order to forge collaborations that incorporate cultural roles and relationships. A careful cross-cultural assessment process can draw from a worker's knowledge about sociocentric versus individualistic cultural orientations, not as a dichotomy but as a continuum in approaching families from cultures or family traditions different than from their own.

3. Workers and administrators steeped in Western human behavior models may tend unwittingly to pathologize ethnic minority cultural

practices and sociocentric family relations. Kinship practices need to be viewed within the given cultural context, without imposing labels such as enmeshed, dependent and codependent in understanding the various relationships and networks. Clinicians need to approach familial traditions and practices as cultural hypotheses (Lopez, 1997) to be explored and appraised for their therapeutic value and the benefit they bring family and cultural preservation.

4. An expanded knowledge of traditions and cultural practices of the extended family network can be incorporated in the development of a comprehensive family approach. Involvement of caregivers as partners in the helping, goal-setting and planning process (Gleeson et al., 1997; Nisivoccia, 1996) is culturally validating of their key role and the function they serve.

5. How is the problem of parental substance abuse perceived? What does it mean to the family network that a family member with such a problem is no longer able to care for young children? Understanding the perceptions and meaning the family members attribute to the situation or crisis is essential to elucidating the cultural context and can guide planning and intervention services.

6. The underutilization of services by older caregivers needs targeted attention (Burnette, 1999a). An assessment of caregiver knowledge of potential or needed resources and services is a required step in meeting a range of social and health needs. What are the unmet needs of the kinship caregiver system? What do these needed services consist of (Goldberg-Glen et al., 1998) and can they be accessed in cultural, local, and age appropriate ways (i.e., advocacy, education, psychoeducation, child development and parenting information, health, mental health, entitlement programs, respite care). The development of viable networks of community supports and peer groups among kinship families may help to meet social needs and strengthen this cultural tradition (Wilhelmus, 1998).

7. As the kinship family system may involve contact with the substance abusing parents, a holistic and ecological comprehensive approach may be possible. This may entail coordination of services from several provider systems of care (i.e., child workers, family therapists, substance abuse treatment workers, health or mental health providers, probation staff) to facilitate permanency planning and therapeutic services.

CONCLUSION

As kinship caregivers absorb the socioeconomic and emotional challenges and life stresses stemming from parental substance abuse, they provide a valuable resource that requires careful appraisal and meaningful support by the provider system. Social service workers need to make a conscious effort to engage in a cultural assessment process according to the concerns raised by several kinship studies, and as suggested by the guidelines of the above framework. Kinship care is a cultural and human resource that is embedded in an existing sociocentric tradition of natural supports afforded to the most vulnerable persons in a family. It is important to appreciate the heritage of kinship care within African American and Latino families in response to the severe consequences of parental substance abuse. However, given the many problems and concerns that have been discussed, it must be emphasized that kinship care as it exists within the formal system of child welfare services should not be idealized. The concerns and limitations that strain kinship caregivers need to be addressed in order to realize the strengths of the investment in this cultural resource.

NOTE

1. The term *Latino* is a broad generalization used to refer to a highly heterogeneous population comprising subgroups of individuals of multiple national origins and distinct immigration histories, who share ancestral ties to Spain and/or indigenous groups of the Americas. Despite its limitations, the term is used to refer collectively to this population provided that its diverse ethnic and cultural origins are acknowledged.

REFERENCES

Baca-Zinn, M. (1994). Adaptation and continuity in Mexican-origin families. In R.L. Taylor (Ed.), *Minority families in the United States: A multicultural perspective* (pp. 66-82). New Jersey: Prentice Hall.

Baldwin, J. A. & Hopkins, R. (1990). African-American and European-American cultural differences as assessed by the world-views paradigm: An empirical analysis. *The Western Journal of African-American Studies, 14*(1) 38-52.

Berrick, J., Barth, R., & Needell, B. (1994). A comparison of kinship foster homes and family foster homes: Implications for kinship as family preservation. *Children and Youth Services Review, 16*, 7-13.

Besharov, D. (1989). The children of crack: Will we protect them? *Public Welfare, 47*, 6-43.

Billingsley, A. (1992). *Climbing Jacob's ladder: The enduring legacy of African-American families*. NY: Simon & Schuster.

Brown, W., & Bailey-Etta, B. (1997). An out-of-home care system in crisis: Implications for African American children in the child welfare system. *Child Welfare, 76*(1), 65-83.

Burnette, D. (1999a). Custodial grandparents in Latino families: Patterns of service use and predictors of unmet needs. *Social Work, 44*(1), 22-34.

Burnette, D. (1999b). Social relationships of Latino grandparent caregivers: A role theory perspective. *The Gerontologist, 39*(1), 49-58.

Bruton, L. M. (1992). Black grandparents rearing children of drug-addicted parents: Stressors, outcomes, and social service needs. *The Gerontologist, 32*, 744-751.

Carrasquillo, H. (1994). The Puerto Rican family. In R.L. Taylor (Ed.), *Minority families in the United States: A multicultural perspective* (pp. 82-94). New Jersey: Prentice Hall.

Carter, C. (1997). Using African-centered principles in family-preservation services. *Families in Society, 78*(5), 531-538.

Children's Defense Fund. (1994). *The state of America's children yearbook*. Washington, DC: Author.

Danzy, J. & Jackson, S. (1997). Family preservation and support services: A missed opportunity for kinship care. *Child Welfare, 76*, 31-44.

Dubowitz, H., Tepper, V., Feigelman, S., Sawyer, R., & Davidson, N. (1990). *The physical and mental health and educational status of children placed with relatives: Final report*. Baltimore: University of Maryland School of Medicine.

du Pont, P. (1997, Oct. 29). A chance to fix foster care. *Tampa Tribune*, p. 15.

Everett, J., Chipungu, S., & Leashore, B. (Eds.). (1991). *Child welfare: An Africentric perspective*. New Brunswick, NJ: Rutgers University Press.

Falicov, C. (1998). *Latino families in therapy: A guide to multi-cultural practice*. New York: Guildford Press.

Falicov, C. (1999). The Latino family cycle. In B. Carter & M. McGoldrick (Eds.), *The expanded family life cycle: Individual, family, and social perspectives* (pp. 141-152). Boston: Allyn & Bacon.

Fuller-Thomson, E., Minkler, M., & Driver, D. (1997). A profile of grandparents raising grandchildren in the United States. *The Gerontologist, 37*(3), 406-411.

Gleeson, J., O'Donnell, J., & Johnson-Bonecutter, F. (1997). Understanding the complexity of practice in kinship foster care. *Child Welfare, 76*, 801-826.

Goldberg-Glen, R., Sands, R. G., Cole, R. D., & Cristofalo, C. (1998). Multigenerational patterns and internal structures in families in which grandparents raise grandchildren. *Families in Society, Sep/Oct*, 477-489.

Hall, D. J. (1998, March 1). Raising their kids' kids doing it all: Again drug abuse by parents is main reason grandparents take on responsibility and burden. *Wisconsin State Journal*, 1A.

Hayslip, B., Shore, R., Henderson, C., & Lambert, P. (1998). Custodial grandparenting and the impact of grandchildren with problems on role satisfaction and role meaning. *The Journal of Gerontology, 53B*, S164-S173.

Hill, R. (1971). *The strengths of Black families*. NY: Emerson Hall.

Ingram, C. (1996). Kinship care: From last resort to first choice. *Child Welfare, 75*(5), 550-566.

Karp, N. (1996). Legal problems of grandparents and other kinship caregivers. *Generations, 20*, 57-60.

Kleinman, A. (1988). *Rethinking psychiatry: From cultural category to personal experience.* NY: Free Press.

Lefley, H. P. (1990). Culture and chronic mental illness. *Hospital and Community Psychiatry, 41*(3), 277-286.

Lewis-Fernandez, & Kleinman, A. (1994). Culture, personality, and psychopathology. *Journal of Abnormal Psychology, 103*(1), 67-71.

Lopez, S. R. (1997). Cultural competence in psychotherapy: A guide for clinicians and their supervisors. In C. E. Walkings, Jr. (Ed.), *Handbook of psychotherapy supervision* (pp. 570-588). NY: John Wiley & Sons, Inc.

Maser, J. D., Cassano, G. B., & Michelini, S. (1997). Treatment implications of comorbid mental disorders. In S. Wetzler & W. C. Sanderson (Ed.), *Treatment strategies for patients with psychiatric comorbidity* (pp. 3-22). NY: John Wiley & Sons, Inc.

McLean, B., & Thomas, R. (1996). Informal and formal kinship care populations: A study in contrasts. *Child Welfare, 75*(5), 489.

Minkler, M., & Roe, K. (1996). Grandparents as surrogate parents. *Generations, 20*, 34-38.

Moore-Hines, P. (1999). The family life cycle of African American families living in poverty. In B. Carter & M. McGoldrick (Eds.), *The expanded family life cycle: Individual, family, and social perspectives* (pp. 327-345). Boston: Allyn & Bacon.

Moore-Hines, P., Garcia-Preto, N., McGoldrick, M., Almeida, R., & Weltman, S. (1999). Culture and the family cycle. In B. Carter & M. McGoldrick (Eds.), *The expanded family life cycle: Individual, family, and social perspectives* (pp. 69-87). Boston Allyn & Bacon.

Morrison-Dore, M., & Doris, J. M. (1998). Preventing child placement in substance-abusing families: Research-informed practice. *Child Welfare, 77*(4), 407-426.

National Institution on Drug Abuse. (1999, May 12). *Information on common drugs of abuse* [Online]. Available: http://www.nida.nih.gov/DrugAbuse.html [1999, May 23].

Nisivoccia, D. (1996). Working with kinship foster families: Principles for practice. *Community Alternatives, 8*(1), 1-21.

O'Laughlin, M. (1998). A theory of relativity: Kinship foster care may be the key to stopping the pendulum of terminations vs. reunification. *Vanderbilt Law Review, 51*(5), 1427-1457.

Parra, P. A., & Guarnaccia, P. (1998). Ethnicity, culture, and resiliency in caregivers of a seriously mentally ill family member. In H. I. McCubbin, E. A. Thompson et al. (Eds.), *Resiliency in Native American and immigrant families* (pp. 431-450). Thousand Oaks, CA: Sage.

Pearson, J. L., Hunter, A. G., Cook, J. M., Ialongo, N. S., & Kellam, S. G. (1997). Grandmother involvement in child caregiving in an urban community. *The Gerontologist, 37*(5), 650.

Pereleberg, R. J. (1983). Mental illness, family and networks in a London borough:

Two cases studied by an anthropoligist. *Social Science & Medicine*, *17*(8), 481-491.

Pinderhughes, E. (1982). Afro-American families and the victim system. In M. McGoldrick & J. Giordano (Eds.), *Ethnicity and family therapy* (pp. 108-125). NY: Guildford Press.

Pruchno, R. (1999). Raising grandchildren: The experiences of black and white grandmothers. *The Gerontologist*, *39*(2), 209.

Scannapieco, M., & Hegar, R. L. (1999). Kinship foster care in context. In R. L. Heger & M. Scannapieco (Eds.) *Kinship foster care: Policy, practice, and research* (pp. 17-27). NY: Oxford University Press.

Scannapieco, M., Hegar, R. L., & McAlpine, C. (1997). Kinship care and foster care: A comparison of characteristics and outcomes. *Families in Society*, *78*, 480-488.

Shweder, R. A., & Bourne, E. J. (1984). Does the concept of the person vary cross-culturally? In R. A. Shweder & R. A. Levine (Eds.), *Culture theory: Essays on mind, self & emotion* (pp. 158-199). Cambridge, MA: Cambridge University Press.

Smith-Barusch, A., & Steen, P. (1996). Keepers of community in a changing world. *Generations*, *20*, 49-52.

Stack, C. (1974). *All our kin: Strategies for survival in a black community*. NY: Harper & Row.

Stevenson, H. C., & Renard, G. (1993). Trusting ole' wise owls: Therapeutic use of cultural strengths in African-American families. *Professional Psychology: Research & Practice*, *24*(4), 433-442.

Taylor, R. L. (1994a). Minority families and social change. In R. L. Taylor (Ed.), *Minority families in the United States: A multicultural perspective* (pp. 204-248). NJ: Prentice Hall.

United States Bureau of the Census. (1994). *Statistical abstracts of the United States: 1994* (114th ed.). Washington, DC: United States Government Printing Office.

Usher, C., Randolph, K., & Gogan, H. (1999). Placement patterns in foster care. *The Social Service Review*, *73*, 22-36.

Wilhelmus, M. (1998). Mediation in kinship care: Another step in the provision of culturally relevant child welfare services. *Social Work*, *43*(2), 117-126.

The Role of Hawaiian Elders in Substance Abuse Treatment Among Asian/Pacific Islander Women

Paula T. Tanemura Morelli, PhD
Rowena Fong, EdD

SUMMARY. The elders of a culture are often the designated transmitters of long-standing values and ways that define the unique essence of a people. Küpuna (elders) teachings are especially important to Native Hawaiians who have experienced the cumulative effects of cultural imperialism, which has taken their lands, discouraged use of their language and cultural ways, damaged their identity as a people and destroyed their sovereignty.

Modern day cultural imperialism, which universalizes the dominant group's experience and culture, renders minority groups as invisible while marginalizing them (Young, 1990). The chronic stress of this insidious form of oppression can translate into physical, mental health problems which lead to decreased life expectancy (McEwen, 1998; Schulkin, Gold & McEwen, 1998). Statistics on Hawaiians and other Asian/Pacific Islanders in Hawai'i indicate these groups have high rates of health problems and increasing rates of substance abuse (Office of Hawaiian Affairs, 1998).

Paula T. Tanemura Morelli and Rowena Fong are affiliated with the University of Hawai'i at Mänoa, School of Social Work, 2500 Campus Road, Hawai'i Hall 213, Honolulu, Hawai'i 96822 (E-mail: morelli@hawaii.edu).

The authors sincerely thank the participants and staff of the Na Wahine Makalapua Project, the State of Hawai'i, Department of Health–Alcohol, Drug Abuse Division and the Center for Substance Abuse Prevention for their support of this study, Grant number: 3514-05.

[Haworth co-indexing entry note]: "The Role of Hawaiian Elders in Substance Abuse Treatment Among Asian/Pacific Islander Women." Morelli, Paula T. Tanemura, and Rowena Fong. Co-published simultaneously in *Journal of Family Social Work* (The Haworth Press, Inc.) Vol. 4, No. 4, 2000, pp. 33-44; and: *Substance Abuse Issues Among Families in Diverse Populations* (ed: Jorge Delva) The Haworth Press, Inc., 2000, pp. 33-44. Single or multiple copies of this article are available for a fee from The Haworth Document Delivery Service [1-800-342-9678, 9:00 a.m. - 5:00 p.m. (EST). E-mail address: getinfo@haworth pressinc.com].

This article describes the roles and Hawaiian practices of kūpuna who acted as facilitators in the healing of Asian/Pacific Islander pregnant and postpartum women who participated in a culturally based substance abuse treatment program (CBSATP). The findings of a qualitative study, which examined the effectiveness of kūpuna in these roles and their implications for practice are discussed. [*Article copies available for a fee from The Haworth Document Delivery Service: 1-800-342-9678. E-mail address: <getinfo@haworth pressinc.com> Website: <http://www.haworthpressinc.com>*]

KEYWORDS. Substance abuse, Asian/Pacific Islander women, Hawaiian elders

INTRODUCTION

In the Hawaiian culture, kūpuna (plural form; kupuna, singular), family elders or grandparents, are regarded as carriers of the culture and tradition, sources of wisdom and knowledge, and interactive teachers. "It is the kūpuna who can convey a sense of continuity in family structure and a knowledge of and pride in the Hawaiian cultural heritage" writes Hawaiian scholar Mary Kawena Pukui (1972). In most cultures, elders are tacit carriers of long-standing values and ways that define the unique essence of a people's being. Kūpuna teachings are especially important to Native Hawaiians who have experienced the cumulative effects of cultural imperialism, which took their lands, discouraged use of their language and cultural ways, damaged their identity as a people and destroyed their sovereignty. Today this oppression continues in more insidious ways within " . . . the everyday practices of a well-intentioned liberal society" (Young, 1990).

A review of the history of Hawaiian oppression and subjugation is beyond the scope of this discussion, however, the written histories of Hawai'i (Anderson, 1865; Buck, 1993; Daws, 1974; Haas, 1992; Liliuokalani, 1899) provide numerous examples, albeit imbedded in the structure of the times, of the ways in which the continuity of Hawaiian family structure, knowledge and values were threatened with extinction. A critical examination of these histories would reveal the exploitation, marginalization, powerlessness, cultural imperialism and the threat of violence (Young, 1990) that were a part of Hawaiian history.

The hegemony of multi-leveled, systemic oppression in the daily lives of racial, ethnic and other minorities often translates into chronic stress, which can manifest in social, interpersonal, physical and mental health problems that come to be associated with minority groups (Outlaw, 1993). Chronic stress may lead to hypertension, obesity, depression, diabetes, immune failure and metabolic imbalance and other mental or physical problems (McEwen, 1998; Schulkin, Gold & McEwen, 1998).

The Native Hawaiian population, prior to western contact in 1778, was estimated to have been as low as 100,000 (Dye and Komori: using Carbon-14 dating and statistical analysis in Bushnell, 1993) and as high as 800,000 to one million (Stannard, 1989: using archival and archaeological reviews, and comparison studies). One hundred years later, the 1878 census located 44,088 Hawaiians and 3,420 part-Hawaiians (Akau et al., 1998). This dramatic decline in the native population has been attributed to the introduction of diseases which Hawaiians had no resistance to, and the loss of their cultural ways, language, power and identity (Judd, 1998). In 1992, Hawaiians and Hawaiians of mixed ancestry constituted approximately 19.3% (220,747) of Hawai'i's population (Office of Hawaiian Affairs [OHA], 1998). Contemporary Hawaiians suffer from high rates of cancer, diabetes, hypertension and other chronic diseases when compared to non-Hawaiians in the state (OHA, 1998), and the highest mortality rates among major ethnic groups in Hawai'i (Mokuau, Browne & Braun, 1998). The cumulative losses of cultural traditions, customs, and identity combined with " . . . difficulties of reconciling western and Hawaiian values, and the experience of being a disadvantaged minority group in their native land" place Hawaiians at high risk for depression (Crabbe, 1998) and related problems such as substance abuse. In 1993, for example, the prevalence of acute drinking (binge drinking) among Native Hawaiians was highest among all racial and ethnic groups in Hawai'i (OHA, 1998). Between 1987 and 1990, the prevalence of maternal substance abuse was highest among Hawaiian women (145.9 per 10,000) and Asian/Pacific Islander women as a group (Filipino, 31.9; Japanese, 36.7; Chinese, 17.6; Samoan 51.4; Korean 43.3; Vietnamese, 21.5; Guamanian 85.8; and other non-whites 34.6 per 10,000) (OHA, 1998).

In response to the critical need for substance abuse treatment among pregnant and postpartum Asian/Pacific Islander (A/PI) women, heath care and social service providers in a rural community of Hawai'i established a culturally based, women-centered residential treatment program. The program was designed to address barriers that often prevent A/PI women from engaging and completing treatment, such as provision for newborns to live with their mothers, child care while women were in substance abuse treatment, infant health-care services, and parent education classes.

This article describes the roles and Hawaiian practices of kūpuna who facilitated women's healing through a culturally based substance abuse treatment program (CBSATP). A portion of the findings of a qualitative study that evaluated the effectiveness of the CBSATP (Fong and Morelli, 1998) is examined with the primary focus on effectiveness of kūpuna.

KŪPUNA AS FACILITATORS IN A CULTURALLY BASED SUBSTANCE ABUSE TREATMENT PROGRAM (CBSATP)

Kūpuna are the elders of the Hawaiian community from which all tradition is conveyed within the extended family. Kūpuna are teachers; the saying, "oi ka `ak`a na make" (while the eyes are still open), counsels the younger generations to learn from their elders while they are still alive.

Twenty-five kūpuna from the local community volunteered to work with the women in the CBSATP. These five men and twenty women kūpuna ranging in age from 55 to 80 came from all walks of life and willingly gave their time and energy to be directly involved with the women participants. Kūpuna were involved in two major areas of the CBSATP: parent education/skill building and facilitating Hawaiian healing practices.

Skill-building efforts. As part of the A/PI women's group-residence program, kūpuna provided child care, reinforced the teachings of the Hawaiian parenting classes, and acted as counselors/listeners. The Hawaiian parenting classes developed by a kupuna focused on Hawaiian culture, values and spiritual ways to strengthen families. The goals were to increase effective parenting through knowledge and skill building, and to encourage behavior, which reflects the values of the Hawaiian culture. The classes also taught basic skills in feeding, bathing, bonding and disciplining children.

Hawaiian healing practices. Within the CBSATP provided by a community agency treatment team, kūpuna facilitated the Hawaiian healing practices of Ho`oponopono and deep cultural therapy, provided counseling and debriefing after these processes, and consulted with professional treatment team members regarding women's progress. Küpuna appraisal and feedback, based on their experiential knowledge, skills and understanding of Hawaiian healing practices were critical to planning the treatment course for the women in the CBSATP.

A/PI women participated in 20 or more hours per week of culturally based treatment. The program's philosophy emphasized that women be immersed in the treatment process and complete all five treatment phases in order to receive its full benefits. The five treatment phases were modeled after the Native Hawaiian healing practice of ho'oponopono. Ho'oponopono is a method for restoring harmony when conflict exists within and between families; traditionally, it was used within the Hawaiian extended family (Pukui, 1972; Shook, 1985). Ho'oponopono is an ancient and traditional practice, which guides the participant to repentance, forgiveness and reconciliation. It is a problem-solving process, usually facilitated by a kupuna. Ho'oponopono is a complex and potentially lengthy group interaction, which includes prayer, statement of the problem, discussion, confession of wrongdoing, restitution when necessary, forgiveness and release by all parties involved. Ho'oponopono was the foundation for all treatment activities within the CBSATP and considered essential to culturally appropriate substance abuse treatment.

Competencies required at each level of healing were assessed by the küpuna and clinical staff before a woman could be moved forward in the treatment process. At each phase, a detailed explanation of ho'oponopono was provided to the women as they proceeded through treatment. In each phase of treatment, women were required to discuss their progress with a küpuna.

Phase I, Ho'omalu brought the women under the care and protection of the program. It was a time to reflect and examine one's feelings, thoughts, and sensations. The goals of this phase were to participate in a group ho'oponopono with a kupuna and to demonstrate a willingness to be completely open, totally honest and fully committed to the treatment process.

Phase II, Kukulu Kumuhana, involved identifying the problem, and pooling the spiritual and emotional resources of the individuals present to focus on the issue at hand. The goals of this phase were: to understand the nature and extent of the addiction, and the resulting problems; to acknowledge addiction as a problem and the need for treatment; to map-out how to reach one's goals; and to thoroughly understand the rights and responsibilities of treatment, and begin to exercise them.

Phase III, Mahiki-Hihia was a time of discussion, acknowledging feelings, and empathizing with the injured individuals. The goals of this phase were to present all issues without suppressing anything; to identify past and present problematic actions, events, attitudes; to begin taking responsibility for one's own actions and attitudes and all the consequences resulting from them; and to establish an effective working relationship between the woman and her professional counselor.

In phase IV, Hala-Mihi, the original problems were reaffirmed and each individual was expected to be aware of his or her role in the current situation. This was the time for complete, full repentance and forgiveness. The goals of this phase were to take full responsibility for past actions and attitudes; to begin asking for and giving forgiveness, making restitution and amends in order to set things right; to consistently let go of resentments; and to begin a deeper level of personal growth.

Phase V, Kala`oki-Pule Ho`opau began the release of all parties from the burden of the problem. It was the time to sever, cut and separate from the burden both mentally and physically. The pule (prayer) to signify the resolution and end of the process took place over a period of weeks. The goals of this final phase were to resume proper place and role within the family and community; to practice independent living skills and relapse prevention; to learn to live on life's terms; to complete treatment plan and obtain a clinical discharge; and participate in group ho`oponopono with a kūpuna. The final phase ended with Pani: the closing meal and hi`uwai (cleansing), symbolizing the act of purification.

Deep culture therapy. Twice a month, kūpuna facilitated six-hour deep cultural therapy sessions. In these sessions, A/PI women role-played and reenacted Hawaiian legends. The discussion that followed enabled them to deal with their emotional distress and receive the group's support. This process, called mahiki, is described as a time of "peeling away" the hurt and pain, which the injured person feels.

Through the combined efforts of the professional substance abuse counselor and kūpuna facilitation during deep cultural therapy, women in this study reported breakthroughs, which opened the way to behavioral and attitudinal change, and the beginning of recovery from substance abuse. Kūpuna noted two recurring themes among the women during deep culture therapy: lack of self-appreciation and internalized oppression. Agency-conducted client satisfaction surveys, over a three-year period, consistently identified deep culture therapy as the most meaningful part of substance abuse recovery.

STUDY METHODOLOGY

Sample and Data Collection

Using a semi-structured interview guide facilitated by ethnographic interviewing methods a sample of twenty-one A/PI program participants shared their substance abuse treatment narratives in two to four hour interviews. The interview guide was designed to enable the participants to describe their experiences in and perceptions of the CBSATP as well as their concerns and suggestions for improvement. The data examined for this analysis focused on A/PI women's perceptions of kūpuna effectiveness in facilitating parenting education and Hawaiian healing practices.

Forty-nine pregnant or postpartum women participated in the CBSATP between 1992 and 1995. The majority of participants were Hawaiian (65% or 32), 14% were white, 10% Hispanic, 10% Asian and one black individual. Thirty-two of the original participants were located. Twenty-five of the 32 women consented to be interviewed for the fifth year evaluation. Twenty-one A/PI women's narratives were analyzed for this study; four non-A/PI were not included in this analysis. Women in the sample were 20 to 37 years of age and had an average of three children.

Within the sample used for the current analysis, 81% or 17 women reported Hawaiian/Part-Hawaiian as their primary ethnicity followed by 19% (4) Asian and Southeast Asians. Nearly three-fourths (15) of the women were single and a little more than half (12) of the women had graduated from high school. Less than half (8) of the women reported an unstable employment history. Eighty-six percent (18) of the women were court ordered into treatment or referred by Child Protective Services (CPS). Methamphetamine (ice) was the substance used by the majority of women (17) followed by cocaine, alcohol and marijuana.

Study Limitations

This study concentrates on revealing the nature of women's experiences in treatment. It must be emphasized that the small sample size does not permit generalizations to be made about kūpuna effectiveness in substance abuse treatment programs.

Second, due to changes in funding while the program was in progress and the women's varied times of entry into the program, only nine of the women in this sample participated in Hawaiian parenting classes. While all women had some form of contact with kūpuna, not all contact was uniform in quality or amount of time spent with each participant.

Data Analysis

Women's narratives were analyzed using grounded theory coding techniques (Glasser and Strauss, 1967). Feminist perspectives provided the lens through which A/PI women's narratives were acknowledged and validated as essential to understanding treatment-facilitating processes (Harding, 1987; Reinhartz, 1992). The focus was to learn about the women's process of involvement in the program, to better understand what was important in enabling them to remain in the program and what they found important or effective in their treatment. Although analysis of the entire data set revealed a range of factors contributing to program effectiveness from the women's perspectives, the findings presented here focus specifically on participants' responses to kūpuna involvement in the CBSATP.

FINDINGS

Fifteen of the 21 (71%) women in the sample responded to the question regarding the effectiveness of the support, teachings and facilitation of healing that they received from kūpuna. Thirteen of the 15 women (87%) expressed positive perceptions about kūpuna involvement and assistance. They found kūpuna helpful in:

• Aiding their healing through Hawaiian cultural practices
• Building parenting skills
• Listening and giving counsel

- Promoting parent-child bonding
- Teaching about the Hawaiian culture.

In discussing Hawaiian cultural practices guided by kūpuna, participant Pua said, "We would have ho`oponopono . . . and let out all our bad vibes . . . where you just leave all the crap that you went through behind . . . Just throw it away, wash it away, throw it out in the ocean and let it just let go. You know? And that was spiritual . . . it was good." Participant Kehau said, "All that hurt and hate that I had inside . . . after deep cultural therapy, wow, it's awesome, it's like a whole burden lifted out of me. I had a problem stuffing things . . . then it just built up, built up, built up, an before I knew it, I was one big time bomb."

Almost two-thirds (13) of the women felt the Hawaiian parenting classes were helpful in developing: positive parenting skills (bathing, feeding, discipline, positive talk to children, time management, schedule, structuring routines); positive attitudes (developing patience, responsibility, attention-giving); and knowledge (child development, attachment and bonding, child safety, nutrition). In discussing the benefits of Hawaiian parenting classes, which were presented and supported by kūpuna, participant Kai said, " . . . you think you are doing everything right [parenting]. But when I got into the program they taught us how to be responsible parents. That was kind of cool for me."

Women in the program reported that kūpuna were most helpful in listening and giving counsel. Participant Kehau said, "They [kūpuna] listened to me when nobody else would listen. They're the only ones to keep the harmony." Participant Hoku shared, "Sometimes she [kūpuna] would intuitively know what we were thinking and tell us about family life. . . . This helped us to talk to her about our families."

Women found kūpuna helpful in the promotion of parent-child bonding. Participant Lehua stated, "They [kūpuna] made me feel less stressed, they took frustration away. They [kūpuna] were helpful to women and their families, emotionally and spiritually and physically." Participant Moana shared, "They [kūpuna] came to teach us some of the Hawaiian cultural ways, such as bonding with family, how to teach children, how to help others; they were teaching us to be good people."

Kūpuna offered spiritual support and reiterated Hawaiian culture. Participant Lehua said, "We'd sing and start talking about culture, about how the ancient Hawaiians used to live off the land, and spiritual things. If you had burdens or problems for the day or you weren't feeling right, they'd pray on you." Participant Hoku said, "She [kūpuna] would teach us whatever things we wanted to learn; she had time to sit down and talk with us. If we have problems, she would pray with us; we would sit and pray together. Kūpuna were good sources of spirituality."

DISCUSSION

Kūpuna played a vital part in enabling women to participate in this community based substance abuse treatment program and facilitating their recovery. Kūpuna supported the women's participation in substance abuse treatment during the day by providing experienced childcare. They taught the women about Hawaiian ways and values, which in turn contributed to restoring the women's identities and building their confidence about themselves and their parenting skills. At the time of this study, eighty percent (17 of 21) of the women in this sample were substance free for at least two years after leaving the program. The remaining four women continued to be in treatment.

The majority of women who participated in Hawaiian deep cultural therapy with kūpuna reported that the healing practices were instrumental in their recovery process. These practices aided A/PI women in reconnecting with their spirituality, facing their emotional pain, confronting the effects of their substance abuse and beginning the healing process.

The effectiveness of enlisting intergenerational involvement in CBSATPs needs to be studied further. However, the value of interventions that incorporate the cultural ways, life experiences, skills and the caring of our elders should not be underestimated as they have a greater potential for effectiveness among cultural, ethnic and racial minorities (Jelik, 1994; Maypole & Anderson, 1987; Singer & Borrero, 1984). In the case of A/PI women who are substance abusers, the use of interventions that are culturally based and that integrate ways of enabling women to learn from caring elders can aid in substance abuse prevention and provide life-saving modeling for future generations.

CONCLUSION

As social workers we must support all communities in their efforts to nānā i ke kumu (look to the source), the source of their strength and identities. Küpuna who were part of this CBSATP for A/PI women are an example of the ways in which Hawaiian community elders can provide a strong foundation of support and caring to begin the process of healing at the individual level and restoration of cultural identity at the community level. Wherever and whenever possible consulting with küpuna of any culture is an important part of developing cultural competency while integrating strengths and empowerment perspectives.

In 1980, the first Hawai`i State conference of küpuna called together Hawaiian elders to address social and economic problems of the Hawaiian community and to discuss how Hawaiian values and cultural ways might become part of developing solutions (Alu Like, 1980). Similarly, in 1982, a series of four Ho`okanaka (meant to convey the meaning of "standing tall" as Hawaiians) Training Workshops brought together about one hundred people from the State of Hawai`i, the majority were Hawaiian, and included local haole (whites), Japanese and Maori residents who represented a wide array of experiences and ideas (Kanahele, 1986). Their task was to identify important Hawaiian values. Nearly 95 percent of the participants found the workshops valuable beyond their expectations, strongly contributing to a renewed sense of identity, self-discovery and potential; as one participant stated, "It only deepened my yearning for my Hawaiianness" (Kanahele, 1986).

Working intergenerationally with community elders brings together life-energies, resources which include knowledge and experience, motivation and hope that have the potential of restoring cultural identities and creating change toward structural equity within our system.

REFERENCES

Akau, M., Akutagawa, W., Birne, K., Chang, M. L., Kinney, E. S., Nissanka, S., Peters, D., Sagum, R., Soares, D., & Spoehr, H. (1998). Ka Ala Ola Pono: The Native Hawaiian Community's Effort to Heal Itself. *Pacific Health Dialog, 5*(2), 232-238.

Alu Like. (1980). *Proceedings of the First Statewide Conference of Hawaiian Küpuna*. Paper presented at the Ka Leo O Na Küpuna, Kamehameha Schools Honolulu, Hawai`i.

Anderson, R. (1865). *The Hawaiian Islands: Their Progress and Condition Under Missionary Labors*. (3rd ed.). Boston: Gould and Lincoln.

Buck, E. (1993). *Paradise Remade: The Politics of Culture and History in Hawai`i*. Philadelphia: Temple University Press.

Bushnell, O. A. (1993). *The Gifts of Civilization: Germs and Genocide in Hawai`i*. Honolulu: University of Hawaii Press.

Crabbe, K. (1998). Etiology of Depression Among Native Hawaiians. *Pacific Health Dialog, 5*(2), 341-345.

Daws, G. (1974). *Shoal of Time: History of the Hawaiian Islands.* Honolulu: University of Hawai`i Press.

Fong, R., & Morelli, P. (1998). *Fifth Year Evaluation of the Na Wahine Makalapua Pregnant and Postpartum Women and their Infants in Hawai`i Demonstration Grant.* Honolulu: Alcohol & Drug Abuse Division, Hawai`i State Department of Health.

Glasser, B., & Strauss, A. (1967). *The Discovery of Grounded Theory: Strategies for Qualitative Research.* New York: Aldine De Gruyter.

Haas, M. (1992). *Institutional Racism: The Case of Hawaii.* Westport: Praeger.

Harding, S. (1987). Introduction: Is there a feminist method? In S. Harding (Ed.), *Feminism and Methodology* (pp. 1-14). Bloomington: Indiana University Press.

Jilek, W. G. (1994). Traditional Healing in the Prevention and Treatment of Alcohol and Drug Abuse. *Transcultural Psychiatric Research Review, 31*(3), 219-256.

Judd, N. L. K. M. (1998). Laau Lapaau: Herbal healing among contemporary Hawaiian healers. *Pacific Health Dialog, 5*(2), 239-245.

Kanahele, G. (1986). *Ku Kanaka–Stand Tall.* Honolulu: University of Hawai`i Press.

Liliuokalani, L. K. (1899). *Hawai`i's Story.* Boston: Lee and Shepard.

Maypole, D. E., & Anderson, R. B. (1987). Culture Specific Substance Abuse Prevention for Blacks. *Community Mental Health Journal, 23*(2), 135-139.

McEwen, B. (1998). Race and Science Radio Interview. Upper Marlboro: National Public Radio.

Mokuau, N., Browne, C. V., & Braun, K. L. (1998). Na Kupuna in Hawai`i: A review of social and health status, service use and the importance of value-based interventions. *Pacific Health Dialog, 5*(2), 282-289.

Office of Hawaiian Affairs. (1998). *Native Hawaiian Data Book 1998.* Honolulu: Office of Hawaiian Affairs.

Outlaw, F. H. (1993). Stress and Coping: The influence of racism on the cognitive appraisal of processing of African Americans. *Issues in Mental Nursing, 14*, 399-409.

Pukui, M., Haertig, E. W., & Lee, C. (1972). *Nana I Ke Kumu: Look to the source.* (Vol. I). Honolulu: Hui Hanai.

Reinharz, S. (1992). Feminist Interview Research. In S. Reinharz (Ed.), *Feminist Methods in Social Research* (pp. 18-45). New York: Oxford University Press.

Schulkin, J., Gold, P. W., & McEwen, B. (1998). Induction of Corticotropin-Releasing Hormone Gene Expression by Glucocorticoids: Implication for understanding the states of fear and anxiety and allostatic load. *Psychoneuroendocrinology, 23*(3), 219-243.

Shook, E. V. (1985). *Ho`oponopono.* Honolulu: University of Hawai`i Press.

Singer, M., & Borrero, M. (1984). Indigenous treatment for alcoholism: The case of Puerto Rican spiritism. *Medical Anthropology, 8*, 246-273.

Stannard, D. E. (1989). *Before the Horror.* Honolulu: Social Science Research Institute, University of Hawai`i.

Young, I. M. (1990). *Justice and the Politics of Difference.* Princeton: Princeton University Press.

Perceptions of Parental Support by HIV Positive Asian and Pacific Islander American Gay Sons

Kerrily J. Kitano, PhD

SUMMARY. This quantitative/qualitative exploratory study, examined HIV positive gay, Asian/Pacific Islander sons' perceptions of their parents' levels of support. Self-administered questionnaires were disseminated predominantly in San Francisco, to obtain a sample of 33 men identified via a snowball sampling strategy, and supplemented by ten in-depth interviews with subjects and service providers. Results suggest that sons were more likely to make disclosures about their homosexuality and HIV serostatus to their mothers, and perceived them to be more supportive than their fathers. With rare exception, parents found ways to be supportive, and time was identified as the most important facilitator of positive transformation. *[Article copies available for a fee from The Haworth Document Delivery Service: 1-800-342-9678. E-mail address: <getinfo@haworthpressinc.com> Website: <http://www.haworthpressinc.com>]*

KEYWORDS. HIV, Asian and Pacific Islander, social support

INTRODUCTION

For each individual who suffers from AIDS or AIDS-related causes, there are many other people affected by the illness. These

Kerrily J. Kitano is affiliated with the Alcohol Research Group, School of Public Health, University of California, Berkeley, 2000 Hearst Avenue, Suite 300, Berkeley, CA 94709.

[Haworth co-indexing entry note]: "Perceptions of Parental Support by HIV Positive Asian and Pacific Islander American Gay Sons." Kitano, Kerrily J. Co-published simultaneously in *Journal of Family Social Work* (The Haworth Press, Inc.) Vol. 4, No. 4, 2000, pp. 45-60; and: *Substance Abuse Issues Among Families in Diverse Populations* (ed: Jorge Delva) The Haworth Press, Inc., 2000, pp. 45-60. Single or multiple copies of this article are available for a fee from The Haworth Document Delivery Service [1-800-342-9678, 9:00 a.m. - 5:00 p.m. (EST). E-mail address: getinfo@haworthpressinc.com].

include members of a person's family, community, and social network. The profound stigma associated with AIDS reported in all communities has led numbers of HIV positive individuals to conceal their illness while families of individuals who have shared their diagnoses have been challenged to be supportive in the face of embarrassment, ostracism, and shame.

The high degree of association that HIV and AIDS has with homosexuality and intravenous drug use is the source of this shame and stigma, sometimes causing rifts in parent-child relationships at a time when the adult child is most in need of support. While it has been widely acknowledged that the family unit is central to Asian/Pacific Islander Americans, there has been little or no research confirming the existence of parental support in the face of AIDS nor to explore the effect of a stigmatized illness on the strength of this bond.

The focus of this paper is on the act of disclosure, both as being gay and of being HIV positive. Open disclosure, we postulated, serves as indicators of trust and closeness in the parent-child relationship and can influence support experiences. A potential supporter needs knowledge that his/her child is ill to appropriately respond. Unwilling to risk losing their place in the family, many men among our sample chose to withhold their diagnosis. We also examined the coming out and post coming-out experiences qualitatively, among those who were brave enough to do so, in the hopes of locating those moments of positive transition when parents recognize the love for their son regardless of their feelings about his homosexuality.

Social Support and Health

Not all researchers have agreed upon a singular and universal definition for social support, nor on ways to measure this concept. While there are a number of studies endorsing the premise that social support has an ameliorative effect on illness, there are significant studies which fail to find direct effects for both psychological and physical variables (Broadhead et al., 1983). Additionally, causality has never been determined due to the lack of utilizing social support as a dependent variable.

While there is some ambiguity regarding the ameliorative effects of social support, much of the literature affirms its positive effects (Gottlieb, 1983; Gore, 1978; Lazarus & Launier, 1978). Among people living with HIV/AIDS, high levels of social support have been correlated with increased survival time, positive immune response, and a higher quality of life (McGough, 1990; Pilisuk & Froland, 1982). Conversely, the effects of stress and a lack of social support have suggested detrimental effects of health and immune function (Sarason, Levine, Basham, & Sarason, 1983).

Parental Response to a Child with AIDS

Illness tends to strain even well-functioning families (Land, 1992) but if the family was in conflict previous to the illness, then the strain in those kinship systems is exacerbated by the illness (Kelly & Sykes, 1989). Parents who did not know at the time of discovering that their son is sick that he is also gay must deal with the "double death syndrome" referring to the actual impending death as well as the death of an identity of a child they thought they knew.

Many parents are ashamed of their adult child's sexual orientation and become anxious about what to tell neighbors, friends, and other family members becoming "hidden grievers" (Murphy & Perry, 1988). The stress of their harboring the secret hampers resolution of grief as well as affecting their own mental health and well-being. If they are highly religious or morally conflicted about a gay son's "lifestyle," they may reject or withdraw from him, finding it easier not to deal with him. These parents are then left with the decision of whether to "come out" to the rest of their families and communities as parents of a gay child. The stressors and stigma that they face are significant. Many blame themselves for faulty parenting (Kelly & Sykes, 1989; Land, 1992) or find that they must defend themselves against the judgment of others who believe they are bad parents.

Children are not supposed to die before their parents. Parents who outlive their children face unbearable grief and live with the feeling that their existence is part of an unnatural order.

Disclosure of Sexual Orientation to Families

Disclosure of homosexual orientation of gay men to their families documents the act of coming out as a crucial turning point with unpredictable results. Alienation, separation from family, rejection, and extensive family disruption are not uncommon consequences (Saperstein, 1983; Myers, 1982; Ben-Ari, 1986).

At the other end of the spectrum, the coming out experience may also lead to increased intimacy and closeness with parents (Sagir, 1973). There are reports of parents whose initial negative reaction to their child's disclosure of being gay, changes positively over time to acceptance (Berzon, 1979; Borhek, 1983; Switzer & Switzer, 1980).

Data from a secondary analysis of the San Francisco Men's Health Study (Turner, Hays, & Coates, 1993) gathered in 1985 and 1987, suggested that the men who accepted their gay identity were more satisfied with their levels of support and that disclosure of homosexuality could facilitate higher levels of support or incite powerful negative influence in the other direction. The family, as a unit, appeared to be particularly helpful or especially harmful to gay men trying to cope with AIDS in their lives. These findings highlight the importance of the coming out process to family members, with dramatic life-changing consequences. The process of coming out to families has not been studied empirically in the Asian/Pacific Islander community.

Asian/Pacific Islander Attitudes Towards Homosexuality

Although there are some locales and social contexts that tolerate the presence of "gaylike" males, nearly all Asian/Pacific Islander cultures view homosexuality as wrong. Homosexuality is the same word for "deviant" in some Asian cultures (Jue, 1987) and there is no equivalent word in other Asian languages. If the concept doesn't exist in language, than it is difficult to speak of its existence.

Parents believe that their children are being corrupted by western influences by "choosing" to be gay. They cannot comprehend why their son would stray from his expected role nor understand that not only does he not feel that he has chosen his sexual preference, but that he is also likely struggling to come to terms with it. These difficulties are enhanced because an individual's behavior is seen as a reflection on the entire family (Aoki & Ja, 1987; Lee, 1989; Ohnuki-Tierney, 1984; Ho, 1984). Conformity to group norms is valued and expected, and that which differs is viewed as suspect (Sue & Morishima, 1982; Morrow, 1989). Additionally, parents may be concerned with the ending of the family line (Gock, 1994; Jue, 1987) which is threatened, unless there are other siblings who will bear children.

AIDS Among Asian/Pacific Islanders

The non-fiction book, *Honor the Children* (Fumia, 1997) was written about the Nakatani family, who lost two sons to AIDS-related causes. This compelling account may be the only data source that captures the perspective of Asian/Pacific Islander parents throughout the HIV disease process. Their regret, which is painfully documented, was that they were not open and supportive to their gay sons in the way they would be now if they could do it all over again. Their portrait presumably captures the way other families might behave under similar circumstances. Their implicit rejection was sometimes unconscious. The father laments, "I can say with confidence that as uncomfortable as the revelations would have been coming earlier; and as badly as we might have handled them, we would have stuck by our children. But they had heard the words come out of our mouths: faggot, queer. They had drawn other conclusions" (p. 64).

This study, an exploratory investigation with a cross-sectional design utilizing both quantitative and qualitative methods, was the third such effort to study HIV positive Asian/Pacific Islanders and the first to look specifically at the impact of AIDS on family relationships. Some of the struggles as well as some cultural factors that promote resiliency were identified among parents whose children have a socially stigmatized illness.

METHODS

Subjects

The sample for the survey section of this research project was comprised of 33 self-identified gay, HIV positive Asian/Pacific Islander men from Chicago, Los Angeles, and the San Francisco Bay Area. This was a highly educated group with 88% having attended some college and with an average annual income between $30,001-$40,000.

This sample was comprised largely of "late baby-boomers" with an average age of 38 years (S.D. 6.18). Seven racial/ethnic groupings were represented including Filipino (36%), Chinese (6%), Mixed Asian/Pacific Islander (6%), Japanese (4%), Vietnamese (3%), Chamorro (1%) and Korean (1%).

Ethnicity is a self-identified measure. A decision to not limit the study population to a few Asian/Pacific Islander ethnicities was made to maximize the pool of potential participants. Additionally, many Asian/Pacific Islander ethnic groups are underrepresented in social science research such as South Asians, Southeast Asians, and Pacific Islanders. The investigator sought their inclusion.

A total of nineteen individuals participated in the qualitative focus groups and in-depth interviews. In-depth interviews were also conducted with four HIV direct service providers (Chinese, Filipino, Japanese, and Vietnamese) to gain a better understanding of the nature of the parent-adult child relationship in the context of AIDS. Their collective experience spanned over eighteen years, working with over 125 Asian/Pacific Islander men with AIDS and their families.

Sampling

Non-probability sampling methods (snowball and chain referral) were employed to reach this largely unstudied and hard-to-reach population. Three key community leaders who identify with the research population assisted in recruitment of participants.

Surveys were distributed in Chicago, Hilo, Los Angeles, New York City, San Diego, Seattle, Washington, D.C., and predominantly, in San Francisco. A response rate of 16.5% was obtained with 90% coming from the San Francisco Bay Area. Self-addressed stamped envelopes, human subject's approval, informed consent, and acknowledgment of the sensitivity of the material were included in the survey packets.

Focus groups and in-depth face-to-face interviews were all conducted in San Francisco. Signed informed consent forms were mandated. All subjects were paid a stipend as a token of appreciation for their time.

Qualitative Data Analysis

All focus groups, in-depth interviews, and open-ended survey data were transcribed verbatim. A content analysis was performed with data coded into the following categories: pre-coming out issues, coming out as gay, coming out as HIV positive, issues with mother, issues with father, coming-out strategies, post-coming out behavior of parents, and an emphasis on Asian/Pacific Islander cultural issues. The many aspects of the coming out process emerged through grounded theory methodology.

Instrument Development

A focus group of four Asian/Pacific Islander gay-identified HIV positive men from San Francisco was conducted to assist in the development of the survey instrument. Issues regarding disclosure of gay identity and HIV serostatus, and parental expectations were discussed. Responses from this group guided the content of the survey instrument.

A draft instrument was then pilot tested on a group of six gay HIV positive Asian/Pacific Islander men to check for sensitivity and potential offensiveness of the instrument, ease of administration, and general content. Diversity in terms of ethnicity and nativity was attempted as best as could be done in a small group to obtain a variety of perspectives to critique the instrument. Data from these individuals were incorporated into the final instrument.

Subjects were asked whether they had disclosed their homosexuality and positive HIV serostatus to their parents. Multiple choice response categories were given to assess the subject's reasons for having disclosed or not having done so to either or both of his parents, each parent's initial reaction to each disclosure, and each parents' current response to both disclosures.

Standard measures to assess subjects' demographic backgrounds were utilized. Demographic variables to assess the subjects' parents were also included.

RESULTS

Descriptive Data

All 33 subjects were HIV positive. Twelve of these subjects (36%) had known that they were HIV positive for five years or less. Eighteen reported (55%) having known for over five years, with a range of subjects having known from 2-11 years. Three responses were missing.

Eighteen subjects reported having had an AIDS diagnosis at the time of completing the survey. The remaining fifteen were HIV positive, without having had an official AIDS diagnosis.

Twenty-nine subjects reported HIV transmission through sexual contact, one through injection drug use, and three were "unsure" how they contracted the virus.

Disclosure of Gay Identity and HIV Status

Twenty-one subjects (64%) reported that they had disclosed that they were gay to their mothers while twelve (36%) did not. There were considerably fewer subjects who made this disclosure to their fathers.

Nine (27%) reported that they had disclosed that they were gay to their fathers, while twenty-four (73%) had not. Among those that did not disclose, were subjects whose parent had passed away, those who were still planning to come out, and parents who knew that their sons were gay because someone else told them or they found out some other way. The essence of this question centered on the active behavior of specifically coming out as gay.

Qualitative data documented the coming out process, which was complex and anxiety-producing. A number of strategies were generated including: execution of a long-term coming out plan, self-imposed distancing, indirect disclosure, no disclosure, gaining an ally in the family first who would assist in disclosing to other family members, selective disclosure to family members, and creation of a "second" family in the event that outright rejection did occur. Culturally appropriate methods for coming out were also discussed. Many felt that indirect disclosure was the way to go. They said that living with subtleties was genuinely fine and did not conflict with their identities as gay men. They felt that they were being respectful of their parents' abilities to cope while still having their partners and lifestyles acknowledged. They did this by "not being willing to talk about getting married and those subjects" while talking about their plans with their current partners or even the fact that their last partner had died of AIDS related causes. All subjects knew of at least one person who bravely came out to their parents and were rejected outright. This ugly worst-case scenario served to keep fear alive, always standing as a painful reminder of what could happen.

Considerably fewer subjects disclosed their positive HIV serostatus to both parents. Seventeen (52%) reported to have told their mothers, while sixteen (48%) opted not to reveal it. Six (18%) made this disclosure to their fathers and twenty-seven (82%) did not. Their greatest concerns centered on placing undue burden upon their families, having to tell their parents that they were gay (if they hadn't done so already), failing to live up to parental expectations, and feeling like they were failures. One of the most prominent fears documented in this study, centered on knowing who would take care of aging or ailing parents. Understanding the unspoken cultural prescriptions of reciprocal care, they worried that they wouldn't be around to fulfill their responsibilities. One subject reflected, "I regret my dad getting older and less well, as we're not able to talk about his health. He is more concerned about my health than his own."

Factors Associated with Disclosure

Chi-square analyses revealed several significant associations. Subjects who knew that they were HIV positive for longer than five years were more likely to disclose that they were gay to their mothers than those who had known less than five years, χ^2 (1) = 7.5, p < .01. They were also more likely to disclose that they were HIV positive to her, χ^2 (1) = 5.30, p < .05, and to their father, χ^2 (1) = 4.19, p < .05. No differences were found between subjects who had an official AIDS diagnosis and those who did not.

A model was then constructed to look more closely at what factors may contribute to whether or not an adult child would disclose his being gay and being HIV positive to a parent. Logistic regression was conducted utilizing the binary outcomes (yes/no) of subject's disclosure of being gay to his mother, subject's disclosure of being HIV positive to his mother, subject's disclosure of being gay to his father, and subject's disclosure of being HIV positive to his father. Independent variables included length of time knowing that subject was HIV positive (less than five years/five years or longer), the presence or absence of an official AIDS diagnosis, and whether subjects were American-born or foreign-born.

Logistic regression was specifically used to calculate estimated odds-ratios which would tell us how much more likely each variable represented was to make a disclosure than its counterpart. Only the variable "knowing that one was HIV positive for over five years" was a significant predictor of coming out as gay to one's mother, seven times more likely than subjects who had known for less than five years (see Table 1). Two factors predicted disclosure of HIV positive serostatus to mothers: knowing that one is HIV positive for over five years and having been born in the United States. Subjects were nearly seventeen times as likely to disclose that they were HIV positive to their mothers if they were born in the United States than in other countries, and eight times as likely to disclose if they have known they were HIV positive for over five years. The presence or absence of an official AIDS diagnosis had no significant impact. The same analyses were conducted examining disclosure of HIV positive serostatus to fathers with no significant findings.

Reaction to Disclosure

The initial reaction by parents upon finding out that their son is gay was recorded in our survey (see Table 2). Of the 21 mothers in our sample whose sons came out to them, 18 (86%) and 9 (100%) of the fathers were "not supportive." Over half of both mothers and fathers were concerned how other family and community members would react. Over half of the fathers were angry. There were also parents who reacted with great love and support. This usually occurred over time, however, following some adjustment phase.

Qualitative data confirmed survey data, underscoring the intensity of emotion that is evoked in parents upon learning that their son is gay. The full range of experience was documented; from total and complete rejection to full acceptance. In almost all instances, even the most anti-gay parents eventually "came around" when they realized their child was sick. However, there were still a couple of families articulated by our provider group sample, that could not cope at all with having a gay son and rejected their sons outright even as they faced death.

The inadvertent or deliberate disclosure of being HIV positive served as another crucial turning point in the relationship between the

TABLE 1. Factors Contributing to Disclosure of Gay Identity to Mother

Characteristic	Disclosure of Gay Identity		Disclosure of Being HIV+	
	Odds Ratio	95% CI	Odds Ratio	95% CI
American-born	0.25	0.03-1.84	16.92	0.00-0.79
AIDS diagnosed	0.89	0.13-5.67	5.39	0.69-41.76
HIV+ over 5 years	7.09	1.23-40.73	8.39	0.93-75.81

TABLE 2. Initial Reaction by Parents to Son's Gay Disclosure

Characteristic	Mothers (n = 21)		Fathers (n = 9)	
	n	%	n	%
Not supportive	18	86	9	100
Concerned how other family & community members will react	12	57	5	55
Upset/Angry	7	33	5	55
Denial	6	28	0	0
Disapproving/Rejecting	5	24	2	22
Supportive	5	24	0	0

subjects in our sample and their parents. Disclosing HIV serostatus had its own set of unique and difficult issues for families to address. Any child communicating to a parent that he has a severe illness that is likely terminal, regardless of age, upsets the natural order of life and death and can evoke the most intense grief known to humankind. Uncertainty and the fear of being unable to fill expected social functions and roles were the main issues that impacted the subjects' ability to disclose their HIV status.

The overwhelming response by mothers upon finding out that their son is HIV positive was that of sadness, worry, and concern about the reactions of other family and community members (see Table 3). Some of the open-ended responses included, "she wouldn't stop crying," "she blamed everything on my partner," and "she became silent." The most common response from fathers upon learning of their son's HIV positive serostatus was sadness and worry (see Table 3).

The initial response of parents upon learning that their sons are HIV positive varied greatly. Much depended on whether they knew beforehand that their sons were gay. Generally, the parents who already knew this could receive the information of their son's HIV disclosure without the strong negative emotion that clouded other parents' ability to sort out the two disclosures. Parents appeared to need time to process the difficult issues that they were being presented with. How much time they need is not possible to say. This was an individual process with many confounding variables.

Parents who were just learning that their son is gay also had to struggle with all of the difficulties of dealing with this issue. Regardless of how they felt about his homosexuality, the notion that he would

TABLE 3. Initial Reaction by Parents to Son's Disclosure of HIV Serostatus

Characteristic	Mothers (n = 17)		Fathers (n = 6)	
	n	%	n	%
Sadness	15	88	6	100
Worried	13	76	6	100
Concerned how other family & community members will react	11	65	2	33
Denial	3	18	3	50
Angry	2	12	0	0
Depressed	2	12	1	17
Other	4	24	3	50

likely become seriously ill and die became the focus of their attention. Fear and panic were also common responses.

Given an undetermined length of time, several families worked through the discomfort of their feelings and rallied around the subjects in our sample to provide support in the ways they could. Providing support meant different things to different people but the key was that the subjects *perceived* their attention as love and support. Some spoke of how they now received weekly phone calls from a parent, literature on the latest AIDS drug therapies, money, medicinal soups, regular visits, and in the case of one dying man, a visit from his entire family from Asia to spend a week together. They ate, slept, toured, and watched TV together, staying in his one-bedroom condominium.

DISCUSSION

Findings from this study are not surprising. Subjects were generally more comfortable in making disclosures to their mother, and more likely to make disclosures if they knew that they were HIV positive for longer than five years and if they were born in the United States. Having had more time to reflect upon the knowledge of being HIV positive provided more opportunities for coming out. Additionally, there may be a greater sense of urgency on the part of those who were beginning to show HIV related symptoms. Subjects raised in the United States have been exposed to mainstream norms which value direct communication and open confrontation. It is also more likely that parents have been exposed to gay and lesbian individuals and issues, theoretically making it less risky for subjects to come out, than among those whose parents were born and raised in Asia.

CONCLUSIONS

Data from this project articulated the struggles which both Asian/ Pacific Islander parents and the adult children experienced in coming to terms with the son's homosexuality and his being HIV positive. However, some of the limitations of the study limit the generalizability of the findings such as the small sample size and the use of non-probability sampling methods. Also, the questionnaires delved into some very sensitive topic areas that only a select group of individuals would be comfortable in answering.

Nonetheless, important information that can be used when working with this population arose from this study. Specifically, for the adult child, a journey of self-exploration and questioning, beginning from "as long ago as I can remember," as well as strategic planning, were prerequisites for disclosure of his being gay. It took years to build a strong enough inner psychological foundation as well as garner enough outside sources of social support, to risk losing and changing his relationship with his parents. Some accomplished this by distancing themselves from their families of origin and surrounding themselves with other gay men. Others opted to spend time alone, or to remain in close contact with their families, only spilling their "secret" at the time when they were finally ready. The stronger their inner foundation, the greater ease in coming out and living with the consequences of having done so. Some Asian/Pacific Islander men chose to make indirect disclosures to their parents about their being gay. This allowed for families to know the truth while not having to directly acknowledge it. While this method of disclosure was deliberate for most, it evolved naturally and unconsciously for others as a way of coming out within the boundaries of their culture and their parents' capabilities.

Parents needed to go through a parallel process of self-exploration and questioning before they could come to a place of acceptance of their gay son. Once there, they needed more time to develop building a strong inner foundation that allowed them to become comfortable with their new identity as parents of a gay child and to withstand societal prejudice. This was generally easier for mothers than fathers.

This sample was comprised entirely of HIV positive individuals. Thus, the coming out process was complicated by inadvertent and deliberate disclosures of both being gay and of being HIV positive. The strong association that AIDS has with homosexuality linked the two disclosure processes. The issues surrounding each of the disclosure experiences were vastly different, but compounded by one another.

The parental reaction to the news that their son was HIV positive was devastating. The fact that their son was gay at that point in time, was largely overridden by concerns about his health. In some cases, however, parents could not work through their prejudices about his being gay and responded by rejecting him, even in times of great need. Data suggest that parents need time to work through their homophobia so that they can appropriately respond to their terminally ill child.

How much time is needed was not determined. It is hoped that parents can accomplish this while their sons are still healthy.

The literature on social support confirms what we know intuitively and what appears to be commonsense about human relationships; that with love and support, people are healthier, happier, and more likely to be contributing members of society. For those individuals with compromised immune systems, whereby illness is inevitable at some point in time, the need for support is that much greater. To have this support from the people that individuals care about most (i.e., family, friends, and community) is going to have a positive impact on their health and well-being; and conversely, the lack of support or disapproval could easily affect the course of illness and quality of an individual's life in a negative way.

What Social Workers Need to Know in Working with This Population

Working with issues of illness, death, and dying requires deep sensitivity and respect for individual styles of grieving. Practitioners and programs which attempt to work with Asian/Pacific Islander American families with regards to HIV and AIDS are working with strong cultural traditions emphasizing regeneration, deference to elders, hierarchical familial role and duty, and a penchant for keeping problems and emotions private. Recognition of the time and hard work it may take for gay, HIV positive Asian/Pacific Islander men to struggle through their largely involuntary defiance of some of these traditions, is essential in the development of successful programmatic strategies.

The news that parents have a son who is gay is met by not only the loss of an image of a son they thought they knew, but the accompanying loss of a sanctioned image which has now been replaced by one that society views as perverse, sick, and wrong. Many parents themselves are sent "in the closet" in shame as they try to hide and protect their own image as "normal" parents. The strengthening of their own identity as parents of a gay child is an important part of the process leading to total acceptance of their gay son. The news that parents have a son with an illness that will likely lead to death is one of the most heartbreaking experiences a parent can be faced with. Recognition of these difficulties is necessary in creating interventions that reach and are genuinely helpful to them. Linguistically competent approaches, and knowledge of culturally appropriate models for disclosing a positive HIV diagnosis and subsequent disclosure of a gay identity are also fundamental in facilitating positive parent-child relationships among this population.

REFERENCES

Aoki, B. & Ja, D. (1987, August 28). *AIDS and Asian Americans: Psychosocial issues*, Paper presented at the annual meetings of the American Psychological Association, New York.

Ben-Ari, A. (1986). *Coming out to parents: An act of self-disclosure.* Unpublished paper.

Berzon, B. (1979). *Positively gay.* Los Angeles: Mediamix Associates.

Borhek, M.V. (1983). *Coming out to parents.* New York: Pilgrim.

Broadhead, W.E., Kaplan, B., James, S., Wagner, E., Schoenbach, V., Grimson, R., Heyden, S., Tibblin, G., & Gehlbach, S. (1983, May). The epidemiological evidence for a relationship between social support and health. *American Journal of Epidemiology, 117(5)*, 521-537.

Fumia, M. (1997). *Honor thy children: One family's journey to wholeness.* Berkeley: Conari.

Gore, S. (1978). The effect of social support in moderating the health consequences of unemployment. *Journal of Health and Social Behavior, 19(2)*, 157-165.

Gock, T.S. (1994). Acquired Immunodeficiency Syndrome. In N.W.S. Zane, D. T. Takeuchi, and K.N.J. Young (Eds.) *Confronting critical health issues of Asian and Pacific Islander Americans.* London: Sage.

Gottlieb, B. (1983). *Social support strategies: Guidelines for mental health practice.* Beverly Hills: Sage.

Ho, M. K. (1983). *Family therapy with ethnic minorities.* Newbury Park: Sage.

Jue, S. (1987). Identifying and meeting the needs of minority clients with AIDS. In, *Responding to AIDS: Psychosocial Initiatives.* NASW publication.

Kelly, J. & Sykes, P. (1989, May). Helping the helpers: A support group for family members of persons with AIDS. *Social Work, 34*, 239-242.

Land, H. (1992). Stress and coping in AIDS caregivers: Partners, friends, and family members. In H. Land (Ed.) *AIDS: A complete guide to psychosocial intervention*, (199-214). Milwaukee: Family Service America, Inc.

Lazarus, R.S. & Launier, R. (1978). Stress-related transactions between person and environment. In L.A. Pervin & M. Lewis (Eds.). *Perspectives in interactional psychology.* New York: Plenum.

Lee, E. (1989), Assessment and treatment of Chinese-American immigrant families. In G. Saba, B. Karrer, & K. Hardy (Eds.) *Minorities and family therapy.* New York: The Haworth Press, Inc.

McGough, K. (1990). Assessing social support of persons with AIDS. *Oncology Nursing Forum, 17*, 31-35.

Murphy, P. and Perry, K. (1988). Hidden grievers. *Death Studies, 12*, 451-462.

Myers, M.F. (1982). Counseling the parents of young homosexual male patients. *Journal of Homosexuality, 7*, 131-143.

Ohnuki-Tierney, E. (1984). *Illness and culture in contemporary Japan.* Cambridge: Cambridge University Press.

Pilisuk, M., & Froland, C. (1978). Kinship, social networks, social support and health. *Social Science and Medicine, 12B*, 273-280.

Saperstein, S. (1983). Support for gay and lesbian adolescents. In S. Saperstein (Ed.) *The second mile, contemporary approaches in counseling young women.* New Directions for Young Women, Inc.

Switzer, D.K., & Switzer, S. (1980). *Parents of the homosexual.* Philadelphia: Westminster.

Turner, H.A., Hays, R., & Coates, T.J. (1993). Determinants of social support among gay men: The context of AIDS. *Journal of Health and Social Behavior, 34*, 37-53.

Perspectives on Family Substance Abuse: The Voices of Long-Term Al-Anon Members

Linda Richter, PhD
Pinka Chatterji
James Pierce

SUMMARY. Based on a series of in-depth interviews with eleven long-term Al-Anon members, the present article examines the perspectives of family members of alcoholics and relates their views on alcoholism and its effects. The interviews explored a number of issues, including respondents' personal experiences living with an alcoholic, the circumstances that drove them to seek help from Al-Anon, and descriptions of their own and other family members' recovery processes. The study highlights the dramatic effects that substance abuse has on the family members of abusers and draws attention to the need for services and support for individuals living with this problem. *[Article copies available for a fee from The Haworth Document Delivery Service: 1-800-342-9678. E-mail address: <getinfo@haworthpressinc.com> Website: <http://www.haworthpressinc.com>]*

KEYWORDS. Alcoholism, Al-Anon, families, recovery, substance abuse

---

Linda Richter, Pinka Chatterji, and James Pierce are all affiliated with The National Center on Addiction and Substance Abuse, Columbia University, New York, NY.

Address correspondence to: Linda Richter, PhD, The National Center on Addiction and Substance Abuse at Columbia University, 152 West 57th Street, 12th Floor, New York, NY 10019.

Preparation of this article was supported by grants from Primerica Financial Services and the Commonwealth Fund.

[Haworth co-indexing entry note]: "Perspectives on Family Substance Abuse: The Voices of Long-Term Al-Anon Members." Richter, Linda, Pinka Chatterji, and James Pierce. Co-published simultaneously in *Journal of Family Social Work* (The Haworth Press, Inc.) Vol. 4, No. 4, 2000, pp. 61-78; and: *Substance Abuse Issues Among Families in Diverse Populations* (ed: Jorge Delva) The Haworth Press, Inc., 2000, pp. 61-78. Single or multiple copies of this article are available for a fee from The Haworth Document Delivery Service [1-800-342-9678, 9:00 a.m. - 5:00 p.m. (EST). E-mail address: getinfo@haworthpress inc.com].

The first offshoot of Alcoholics Anonymous (AA) was Al-Anon, founded in 1951 for family members of alcoholics. According to Al-Anon's philosophy of recovery, taking part in the program allows the family member to develop a more adaptive self concept, better relations with others, a more accurate and understanding perspective of past family experiences, and a better sense of spirituality (Humphreys, 1996). Al-Anon's description of its own program describes recovery as being based on 12 Steps for personal recovery, 12 Traditions to help "sustain unity and harmony," and 12 Concepts of Service aimed at spreading Al-Anon's message worldwide. These 12-step concepts have been adapted from the AA program (Al-Anon Family Groups, Inc. 1979).

Central to Al-Anon's approach is its belief in a disease model of alcoholism, and the corollary notion that family members are powerless over alcoholism and its effects. Thus, a major aim of Al-Anon is to teach "detachment" from alcoholism; members must learn that they have no control, are not responsible, and are not to be blamed for the alcoholic family member's drinking or consequent behavior (Ablon, 1974). Al-Anon members have reported that the group meetings help them openly discuss their feelings, provide them with an intellectual understanding of alcoholism and its consequences, enhance their adaptive coping skills, and expand their social network (Kurtz, 1994). There is also a strong element of spirituality in the program, such that members are encouraged to rely on a higher spiritual power. This "turning one's life over to a power greater than one's self" relates to the notion that Al-Anon members must try to acknowledge that they themselves are not in control of alcoholism, are not responsible for it, and must detach themselves from any blame (Al-Anon Family Groups, Inc. 1979). Another essential component of Al-Anon is the provision of social support among group members (Collins, 1990). Group members "share" their stories and reach out to one another in times of need. Finally, Al-Anon members are taught practical strategies for dealing with an alcoholic family member.

PREVIOUS RESEARCH

Although Al-Anon is one of the largest programs available for families with an alcoholic member, research literature addressing its efficacy is scarce (Keinz, Schwartz, Trench, & Houlihan, 1995). Several studies, however, have attempted to examine the relationship between Al-Anon membership and certain components of adaptive life functioning. For example, in interviewing 20 highly involved members of Adult Children of Alcoholics, a group nested within the structure of Al-Anon, Humphreys (1996) attempted to trace transformations in members' perceptions of their alcoholic families of origin over time. In general, new members tended to see their families as relatively normal but then came to see them as more pathological and dysfunctional over time. Members begin to place responsibility on the disease of alcoholism itself, and alcoholic parents are eventually seen as victims of the disease who should be grieved rather than condemned.

McBride (1991) surveyed 50 members of AA to test the hypothesis that those who had a family member attending Al-Anon would report less family stress than would those with no family member attending Al-Anon. The findings revealed that (1) the longer a family member had attended Al-Anon, the lower the reported stress of both the AA member and the Al-Anon member; and (2) AA members who had a family member in Al-Anon had a significantly higher rate of continuous attendance at AA.

Finally, Keinz et al. (1995) attempted to evaluate the benefits of Al-Anon by examining measures of self-esteem and marital adjustment among a sample of members. Keinz et al. hypothesized that the length of membership in Al-Anon would be positively related to measures of self-esteem and marital adjustment. The findings from this study indicated that while there was a significant positive correlation between self-esteem and length of membership in Al-Anon, age was a confounding variable in this relationship. A more convincing relationship between length of membership and marital adjustment was found in this study, such that a greater length of time as an Al-Anon member was associated with greater overall marital adjustment.

It is important to note that the majority of the studies that have investigated the effects of Al-Anon on its members have been cross-sectional in design. Such cross-sectional studies preclude any conclusions of causal association between Al-Anon membership and positive outcomes or the drawing of inferences regarding the timing of events among variables assessed in the respective studies.

To date, the empirical findings regarding the efficacy of Al-Anon are limited, yet somewhat consistent in their finding that Al-Anon does seem to help members recover from the effects of having an alcoholic family member. Few studies, however, have attempted to understand the multiple and complex life experiences that impel an individual to reach out to a program such as Al-Anon, the components of Al-Anon that seem to resonate most with its members, or how Al-Anon influences members' adjustment and well-being. Such information can be gleaned from in-depth interviews with some of Al-Anon's most devoted, long-term members.

THE PRESENT STUDY

The aim of the present study was to qualitatively examine how Al-Anon members, primarily partners of alcoholics, describe their experiences living with substance abuse in the family and their experiences with the Al-Anon recovery process. The interviews were conducted on a select group of Al-Anon members, as will be described below, and therefore, the findings should not be generalized to other family members of substance abusers. Our aim in this article was to attain from some Al-Anon members a sense of what it is like to have an alcoholic family member and what steps one might take to deal with the problem of alcoholism in the family.

METHOD

This analysis was based on semi-structured interviews conducted with eleven Al-Anon delegates, trustees, and World Service Organization (WSO) staff who were attending the annual Al-Anon World Service Conference held in Stamford, CT in April, 1999.[1] The Al-Anon WSO helped to identify potential interview respondents by contacting delegates who confirmed that they would be arriving early to the conference. The potential respondents were asked if they would be willing to participate in taped, hour-long interviews focusing on Al-Anon and the family recovery process. All of the potential respondents that were approached agreed to participate and gave their informed consent at the time of the interview.

Each interview was conducted in a small hotel conference room with two interviewers using a loosely structured survey instrument.[2] The two interviewers were African-American and Asian-American in their late twenties. The instrument consisted of open-ended, general questions in three areas: (1) coping with a family member's substance-abuse problem; (2) the impact of substance abuse on the family; and (3) the recovery process and the role of Al-Anon in that process. Respondents also were encouraged to discuss any specific Al-Anon tools and resources that they found particularly important in the recovery process. Each interview lasted approximately one hour.

The eleven respondents who were available for interviews were mostly female, white, middle-aged and relatively well educated. Most respondents had initiated Al-Anon membership because of a spouse's alcohol problem. All respondents were long-term, active members of Al-Anon who were delegates, trustees, or WSO staff members for the national Al-Anon conference. The number of interview respondents was limited by time and space constraints at the conference. The demographic composition of this small, non-random sample, therefore, is not representative of all Al-Anon delegates, trustees, or WSO staff, or of Al-Anon membership as a whole. Consequently, no attempt is made in this analysis to generalize from the interviews to a larger population. Instead, the objective of the analysis is to better understand pathways to family recovery from a select group of Al-Anon members' experiences.

RESULTS

Respondents generally appeared comfortable discussing their experiences with the Al-Anon recovery process and, more generally, discussing their experiences as family members of alcoholics. Although respondents were not asked to reveal the nature of their relation to the alcoholic (i.e., partner, parent, child), all did in the course of the interview. In many cases, the respondent was no longer living with the substance-abusing family member, and in several cases there was more than one alcoholic in the respondent's family.

Early Signs of Substance Abuse

Most respondents could not identify a particular event or experience that made them realize that their family member had a problem with alcohol. From the family member's perspective, the onset of problems appeared to be gradual and increasingly troubling.

> . . . *I would have a drink too, but I usually stopped at one or two and [the family member]*[3] *didn't. After a period of time, it be-*

came more difficult. It just wasn't fun and you start noticing that. You don't realize that there really is a problem. You just kind of gradually notice it . . . It wasn't like you wake up one morning and you say, I'm living with an alcoholic . . .

. . . [it was] definitely progressive . . . we'd go out or to a party or have people in or whatever, and [the family member] would drink and I wouldn't notice that [the family member] was drinking. And then I would begin to count. I noticed that as [the family member] drank, [the family member's] behavior changed . . .

. . . it started out just drinking a little. Then it progressed to being gone three and four days at a time.

Most respondents noted that, in retrospect, there had been warning signs that their family member had a problem with alcohol. In some cases, these signs were subtle while in other cases respondents could only recall crisis situations that brought the problem to their attention.

. . . [the family member] started getting arrested a lot. I mean that was a pretty good indication.

. . . there was a series of hospitalizations . . . One time the car rolled over . . . A total of 5 cars totaled and hospitalizations and stuff like that.

. . . [the family member] just drank and was drunk for like a week, and I knew right away . . .

Some respondents described themselves as being in denial, indicating that they may have deliberately overlooked or misread early signs that would have suggested a problem.

. . . [the family member] was telling me for years before I believed it . . . the denial was pretty strong

I was in denial. I didn't want to believe that this was really happening.

The signs were there. I just didn't realize, I didn't know how to read them . . . The only time I can remember ever thinking about the fact that there was alcohol involved was the fact that no matter what [the family member] went to the store for, [the family member] came back with a bottle. And just alcoholism wasn't something that occurred to me.

I really, truly didn't know it was happening. And [the family member] didn't go to bars. [The family member] sat at home and drank and got drunk . . . it all makes no sense when I look back on it, you know. But it was true; I was such a good pretender, I just didn't even look at it.

You get really good at pretending, making things up . . . I just pretended like it wasn't happening.

Consequences of Substance Abuse on the Family

Respondents reported that initially they dealt with their family member's substance abuse in a variety of ways, including ignoring or denying the problem, nagging the substance abuser, trying to conceal the problem from others, and seeking treatment and help. Many respondents initially reacted to the problem with strong emotional responses, such as feelings of anger, frustration, helplessness, embarrassment, and anxiousness.

I got angry but didn't say anything. I had a lot of resentments . . . I spent a great deal of my life before Al-Anon angry.

I wanted to slap [the family member]. I thought, straighten up, behave yourself.

Well, I just, I always would feel frustrated if I would talk with [the family member] at all about [the family member's] drinking and . . . [the family member] would say [the family member] doesn't have a problem and it would only cause more problems between us . . .

I took [the family member] away from family gatherings before [the family member] got drunk so they wouldn't know, because as I said, there was . . . stigma.

As respondents came to acknowledge the severity of the problem, thoughts related to the problem began to fully occupy their thoughts and actions.

> *. . . over a period of time it becomes the main focus of my life that [the family member]was drinking too much . . . you keep focusing on it and it becomes a bigger and bigger and bigger picture until that's all that you think about. I would be at work and all I can think about was what was happening with [the family member]. You know, so my whole focus was on the alcoholic.*

> *[The family member] said something rotten to me and it would be in my thoughts all day long. I would obsess about something [the family member] said.*

> *Well, I didn't deal with it very well . . . when the responsibility became mine, there is an enormous amount of anxiety and all of that's going along with it, you know the fear of what's going on, the constant worry, the constant focus on the other person.*

Many of the respondents initially described a sense of responsibility for the alcoholic's problem. They also reported feeling embarrassed about not being able to help keep the problem under control. More specifically, a general theme that emerged repeatedly was that many of the respondents felt the need to be in full control of the situation and that every instance of drinking by the alcoholic family member was evidence of their own failure to keep the situation under control.

> *. . . pretty soon the idea in my mind is, if I can find the right thing to say, . . . the right whatever, then I can get this to stop. So now it has become my responsibility. You know it never occurred to me that the natural progression would be that [the family member] would keep drinking no matter what. I thought there was some-thing I should be doing that would help this person.*

> *During the drinking years I tried to control the alcoholism . . . I thought it was my fault and I thought it was my responsibility to put up with all this . . . I had to do everything to make [the family member] happy because then maybe [the family member] wouldn't drink.*

I tried to do all the right things and make the house right and do everything to make it a perfect little family so that [the family member] wouldn't drink.

I wanted to be perfect so everything would be okay at home.

A corollary theme that emerged from the interviews was that a number of the respondents described themselves as having low self-esteem and trying to gain feelings of self worth by helping the substance abuser. Furthermore, their inability to help just damaged their self-esteem even more, making them feel like failures.

I thought everything was my fault. Like if I were in a store somewhere and you stepped on my foot, I would say excuse me, I must have been in your way. I mean, everything was my fault.

Self-esteem seems to go away. I'm not sure but I think it has something to do with feeling responsible for [the family member] and not having the success of being able to help.

Those of us who are attracted to alcoholics are caretakers, nurturers. And we get our feelings of self worth not from who we are, but what we can do for other people . . .

This notion of being responsible for the problem and, given sufficient effort, capable of controlling it, is one that is particularly targeted by the Al-Anon program.

Regardless of how the they coped with an alcoholic family member, all respondents felt that substance abuse had a serious and sometimes devastating impact on themselves and other family members. Some reported experiencing physical symptoms of illness in response to the stress associated with having an alcoholic family member.

I felt very depressed. I suffered from anxiety attacks.

I exhibited signs of the inability to eat or to concentrate. I couldn't eat and I was shaking inside all the time and it all had to do with the alcoholism. And the not eating and the running of the marathons, it was like . . . this is one area of my life I can control. I can't control any of this other stuff, but I can control this.

> *. . . The effects of [alcoholism] can be disastrous. I know time after time that physically women get ill . . . Where the stress affected me was in my gums. I had to go to a periodontist.*

Respondents described their own and other family members' feelings of fear, anxiety, anger, and depression, and having to endure constant arguing and abuse, both verbal and physical.

> *. . . [the family member] came home and I got angry because [the family member] was inebriated . . . and I found out later that [the family member] was in a blackout . . . [the family member] started whacking me on the head . . . [the family member] lost control and went to choke me. . . . grabbed my throat and threw me to the ground.*

> *I felt crazy. I didn't know what to do . . . I felt very depressed. I suffered from anxiety attacks . . . the doctor, you know, told me to take the pills and take a rest and take it easy. But it's very hard to take it easy when you live with an alcoholic.*

> *. . . I was going absolutely nuts. You know, like I said, I was having anxiety attacks, I was constantly worried, I wasn't being productive as I could have been . . .*

> *I never knew how I was going to feel when I woke up in the morning until I saw how the alcoholic felt. That means if [the family member] was happy, I was happy. If [the family member] was depressed, I was depressed. I was sort of the caboose attached to the alcoholic engine.*

Many expressed the heightened fear and anxiety associated with the substance abuser's erratic behavior and unpredictable outbursts of anger and violence.

> *. . . I was scared to death. I didn't know what in the world was going to ensue that night, whether we would be in a good mood or not in a good mood . . . I guess fear would be the biggest emotion that I had at that time . . .*

> *. . . [the family member would] get drunk and so you walk on eggshells, and you watch what you say, and you watch what you do . . . there is no way to please . . .*

When [the family member] would come home, it didn't matter how we reacted, a fight would ensue, an argument, sometimes it got violent, sometimes it didn't. It didn't seem to matter if we didn't say anything or if we said a lot. Whichever, we did the wrong thing as far as [the family member] was concerned. Whichever way we reacted, that was another excuse for [the family member] to go back out and drink.

Children suffered by having an alcoholic parent in a variety of ways. Many respondents reported that children were very much affected by the emotional and/or physical absence of the substance abusing family member.

[The family member] wasn't there, [the family member] was out drinking, and I didn't have [the family member] to take it out on at times and I would be angry with [the children] and scream and holler. [The children] were ashamed. They got to the point where they wouldn't have their friends over.

[The family member] didn't participate in the family at all . . .

In addition, several respondents noted that children's roles developed around the substance-abuse problem, with older children sometimes becoming caretakers for younger children.

. . . the oldest became a mother to the middle one and the youngest one. And she would really take care of them . . . giving up that role was hard for her.

Parental roles also were affected by substance abuse; in some cases, the sober parent became a controlling disciplinarian while in other cases the sober parent over-compensated for the substance abusing parent's absence, acting as a martyr.

I became very controlling, very strong as a mother . . . I mean, the children all depended on me to do everything. I did everything for everybody. I could solve any problem, do anything . . . [I] really stripped [the family member] of integrity, took it away because I didn't trust [the family member] to do anything so I just did everything. I think the children probably felt sorry for [the family member] and blamed me more.

You know, I had to cook and wash the clothes and all that stuff, you know. And I guess with my being affected by it, you know, I was the mean one. I was the mean parent between the two of us . . . I guess I was holding in all these emotions and I just kind of took it out on [the child].

. . . the oldest grew up angry and probably [there] wasn't enough real discipline. It was a lot of yelling and screaming like I got when I was a kid. Not very much real punishment . . . and the kids sort of wanted to do what they wanted to do.

It's damaging your children by saying, Oh no, honey, you didn't hear that last night. You must have had a bad dream . . . Why, no, there's nothing wrong. And as their mother, I should have been the one they turned to for the truth. Children who are lied to like that grow up doubting their judgment, doubting their senses . . .

Everybody sort of grew up separately. We were not close. Nobody talked.

The Family Recovery Process

Respondents were asked to describe the recovery process and the impact of the recovery process on family members. They also were asked about the main factors that were responsible for their successful recovery as a family. Some respondents focused on their own recovery, while others mainly discussed the substance abuser's recovery.

Some respondents reported strong resistance to seeking help for themselves in dealing with the alcoholic family member. They felt resentful that they should have to go into treatment because somebody else had a drinking problem.

So in my mind, I'm sitting there . . . and they're telling me that I am sick, . . . and that I need to go through treatment. And I'm thinking, you guys are absolutely crazy. I'm okay. I'm the one who kept it all together . . . I was shaking and falling apart myself, but in my mind I was keeping everything together.

I would support this new sobriety by saying, see what I am doing for you. And I didn't think I needed Al-Anon. I didn't realize how sick I was.

Although respondents were not asked specifically to discuss Al-Anon at this time, many described (and praised) the tools and services offered through the program, and they generally felt that Al-Anon served a critical role in their recovery. Many felt that it was the first time that their own needs were being addressed, rather than those of the alcoholic. Respondents perceived Al-Anon's role in the recovery process as quite beneficial, particularly in terms of its provision of social support, and its focus on removing the blame and responsibility from one's self.

> *At first it was like being wrapped in a warm bubble . . .*

> *. . . it clicked . . . I don't know what they said, but I felt at home. People seemed to understand. They weren't accusing me of anything or whatever, they just knew. They had been through it.*

> *I go to meetings and it's that personal contact in being able to speak privately with people and talk about how I feel with somebody that understands and relates to it.*

Still, many of the respondents reported having much difficulty during the recovery process as well.

> *I wish I could tell you it all became sweetness and light. It did not. It had been so easy to blame everything on [the family member's] drinking. You know, next to an alcoholic, anyone looks good.*

> *With alcoholics, their sobriety comes first, not you. And it was a very tough thing for me to accept that after all this time, I still was not #1. So I got sicker coming to Al-Anon while the alcoholic got better going to AA.*

> *. . . our children did not like us getting in recovery at all . . . They would have never said that but we weren't doing for them all the things that we had been doing for them, particularly me. I wasn't responsible for their behavior any longer . . .*

The Al-Anon notion of giving one's life over to a "higher power" taps into the feeling that many family members of alcoholics have of being responsible and needing to be in full control.

> *... when we turn something over to God, we're not abandoning it. We are turning the person or situation over to God who loves them more than we can.*

One of the main lessons taught by Al-Anon is that family members of alcoholics are not responsible for the illness and that they must detach themselves and stop trying to control everything around them and just focus on their own lives.

> *I was able to let go. I was able to let the alcoholic recover. It was none of my business. I didn't cause it, I couldn't control it, and I can't cure it.*

> *The biggest thing I learned probably is that I'm here to live my own life and do what's best for me, to take care of myself. And it's not my job to take care of the world and fix everybody around me and make everybody happy. My job is my own happiness and my own well being ...*

> *I told [the family member] that I work my program and you work yours and there's no "us" recovery.*

Needs of Family Members of Alcoholics

Respondents were asked to comment on what message they would deliver, given the opportunity, to someone who was in a position to influence social policy (e.g., a government official) with regard to alcoholism and treatment for family members of alcoholics. The majority of respondents expressed the importance of educating the public that alcoholism is a disease and has wide-reaching effects and that there are programs, such as Al-Anon that can really help.

> *I would try to educate them ... what had the best results? Who are the most emotionally sane families of alcoholics?*

> *Hopefully they could support any efforts, public information efforts that go into bringing the message to the public. There are a lot of people who are suffering as a result of alcoholism. Women who are abused, usually alcohol is involved, so hopefully they would support shelters and things like that.*

There really isn't enough education on the subject of substance abuse. And we do a lot of interdiction and we do a lot of things about how bad drugs are, but there is one socially acceptable drug and that's alcohol. We need to educate people that the help is there if you need it. If you take all the money that you spend on interdictions and spend it on education, you may have fewer people using than you do now. Educate people to realize the symptoms. To realize what's going on . . . and where the help is . . . that there are programs to help people in those situations.

I would encourage them to come [to AA and Al-Anon meetings] and hear people's stories and know what they've been going through and to please make people aware if they can of both of these programs.

One respondent expressed the importance of focusing more on the root of the problem–adult substance abuse, rather than putting all the resources in children, whom would not need as much help if the adults in their lives were not substance abusers.

. . . I think like 30% [of our substance abuse funding] should be going to the children and 70% should be going to the adults who have the problem because these children are living with it. And we can do whatever we want . . . we can take a whole school day or 8 hours, but there are still 16 hours left when they're at home living with the problem.

DISCUSSION

The discussions with the respondents clearly suggest that, for those members who were interviewed for this study, Al-Anon was a major factor in their improvement and in their ability to deal with having an alcoholic family member. Several consistent themes emerged from the interviews. The realization that one is living with an alcoholic is one that would be expected to happen quite quickly, given that most of the respondents had prior experiences living with an alcoholic (i.e., parent or spouse). Most admitted that there were numerous signs that the family member's substance use was becoming problematic. Nevertheless, most described the realization as one that was gradual, probably delayed to some extent by the respondents' denial of the problem.

Once the alcoholism became a main factor in the respondents' day-to-day existence, there were numerous and often devastating circumstances for the family members. Respondents often reported instances of emotional and physical absence and abuse from the alcoholic family member, and frequent feelings of embarrassment, anxiety, anger, and despair. A theme that was repeated throughout the interviews was that family members of alcoholics are often low in self-esteem and feel that they are somehow responsible for both the family member's abuse of substances and for his or her eventual recovery. This sense of needing to exert control over all aspects of the family situation is quite a burden for the family members of substance abusers.

> *The family of the alcoholic is dealing with a lot of those same problems that are caused by the disease of alcoholism without the anesthetic of the alcohol.*

Many of the respondents reported that this burden was lifted to some extent once they joined Al-Anon and learned that they were responsible only for their own happiness and well-being. According to the respondents, Al-Anon helped reduce much of the emotional stress by providing the family members of alcoholics with unconditional social support and acceptance, and by providing them with the spiritual means to turn over their feelings of control and responsibility to a "spiritual power" greater than themselves.

The results presented in this article are based on a limited number of interviews with a select group of family members of substance abusers. More specifically, the interviews were restricted to those members of Al-Anon who were clearly impressed by the program to the extent that they remained long-term members and volunteered as delegates or trustees to represent the program at Al-Anon's national and World Service Conference. As a consequence, the findings from this sample do not allow for evaluations of members who might have viewed the Al-Anon program as unhelpful and chose to drop out. In addition, the respondents were mostly female, white, and middle-aged, further limiting the generalizability of the findings to other groups. For all these reasons, caution must be exercised when generalizing these findings to other family members of substance abusers. The advantage of our sample, however, is that these long-term members are more likely than individuals who were only peripherally involved in the program to have experienced the full range of Al-Anon's advantages and disadvantages and could probably provide a more accurate appraisal of the program's overall strengths and weaknesses (Humphreys, 1996).

Implications for Research and Training

The results of this analysis highlight the need to educate future social workers about the diverse ways in which substance abuse affects the entire family system and not just the substance abuser. Social work training programs should include exposure to family-based treatment strategies. These treatment strategies should focus not only on ways in which family members can assist the substance abuser in recovery, but also on helping the family members themselves overcome the problems they face as a result of living with a substance abuser. Furthermore, social work training programs should address the potentially important role of family self-help groups such as Al-Anon.

Future research should examine the perspectives of a more diverse group of Al-Anon members in order to gain a more comprehensive understanding of their experiences and world views both in relation to Al-Anon and, more generally, in relation to living with substance abuse.

NOTES

1. A twelfth interview was conducted but the results could not be used because of the malfunctioning of a tape recorder.

2. The instrument is available from the authors by request.

3. To protect the anonymity of the respondents and their families, we replaced all pronouns describing the alcoholic family member (mostly those referring to the sex of the substance abuser) with "the family member."

REFERENCES

Ablon, J. (1974). Al-Anon family groups: Impetus for learning and change through the presentation of alternatives. *American Journal of Pychotherapy, 28*, 30-45.

Al-Anon Family Groups, Inc. (1979). *Al-Anon speaks out*. Al-Anon Family Group Headquarters, Inc.

Collins, R. L. (1990). Family treatment of alcohol abuse: Behavioral and systems perspectives. In R. L. Collins, K. E. Leonard, & J. S. Searles (eds.), *Alcohol and family: Research and clinical perspectives* (pp. 285-308). New York: Guilford Press.

Humphreys, K. (1996). World view change in adult children of alcoholics. Al-Anon self-help groups: Reconstructing the alcoholic family. *International Journal of Group Psychotherapy, 46*(2), 255-263.

Keinz, L. A., Schwartz, C. S., Trench, B. M., & Houlihan, D. D. (1995). An assessment of membership benefits in the Al-Anon program. *Alcoholism Treatment Quarterly, 12*(4), 31-38.

Kurtz, L. F. (1994). Self-help groups for families with mental illness or alcoholism. In T. J. Powell (Ed.), *Understanding the self-help organization: Frameworks and findings* (pp. 293-313). London: Sage Publications.

McBride, J. L. (1991). Assessing the Al-Anon Component of Alcoholics Anonymous. *Alcoholism Treatment Quarterly, 8*(4), 57-65.

Effects of Family Involvement on Length of Stay and Treatment Completion Rates with Cocaine and Alcohol Abusers

Deni Carise, PhD

SUMMARY. Substance abuse is a problem of national concern. This study sought to replicate and further develop findings from a previous study that found cocaine abusers continued in and completed treatment less frequently than alcohol abusers, and that family involvement may influence continuation in and completion of treatment for both cocaine and alcohol abusers.

A sample of 99 primary cocaine abusers and 105 primary alcohol abusers in outpatient treatment were followed during the course of their treatment. Results indicated primary alcohol abusers were significantly more successful in completing treatment than primary cocaine abusers. Family involvement in treatment significantly increased the likelihood that cocaine and alcohol abusers would complete the full course of treatment.

It is possible that treatment could be improved and completion rates increased by coordinating the involvement of the family. *[Article copies*

Deni Carise is affiliated with The Treatment Research Institute, University of Pennsylvania, Philadelphia, PA.

Address correspondence to: Deni Carise, The Treatment Research Institute, 600 Public Ledger Building, 150 South Independence Mall West, Philadelphia, PA 19106-3475 (E-mail: dcarise@tresearch.com).

The author wishes to acknowledge the assistance of Drs. Robert Forman, Arthur Nezu, Laura McNicholas and A. Thomas McLellan.

The National Institute on Drug Abuse (NIDA training grant T-32-DA07241-04), the University of Pennsylvania/Veterans Administration Center for Studies of Addiction, and the Office of National Drug Control Policy provided support for this project.

[Haworth co-indexing entry note]: "Effects of Family Involvement on Length of Stay and Treatment Completion Rates with Cocaine and Alcohol Abusers." Carise, Deni. Co-published simultaneously in *Journal of Family Social Work* (The Haworth Press, Inc.) Vol. 4, No. 4, 2000, pp. 79-94; and: *Substance Abuse Issues Among Families in Diverse Populations* (ed: Jorge Delva) The Haworth Press, Inc., 2000, pp. 79-94. Single or multiple copies of this article are available for a fee from The Haworth Document Delivery Service [1-800-342-9678, 9:00 a.m. - 5:00 p.m. (EST). E-mail address: getinfo@haworthpressinc.com].

79

available for a fee from The Haworth Document Delivery Service: 1-800-342-9678. E-mail address: <getinfo@haworthpressinc.com> Website: <http://www.haworthpressinc.com>]

KEYWORDS. Treatment, family, outcomes

INTRODUCTION

Substance abuse and its treatment is a $150 billion per year industry in our nation (Pettinati, 1990). With an estimated 10 million Americans experiencing problematic use of alcohol and an estimated 4.8 million Americans abusing cocaine, this expenditure occurs in many forms. Federal, state, and corporate funding is depleted by a myriad of diverse costs. Funds are provided for such assorted needs as disability payments, unemployed individuals, and hospital medical problems. The federal drug control budget was 17.9 billion in 1999 and the economic costs relating to alcohol and drug abuse are estimated at $377 billion in 1995 (ONDCP, Sept. 1999).

In the time period between 1970 and 1990, the fastest growing substance abuse problem in our nation was cocaine use, particularly in the form of "crack" cocaine. Crack was called "the newest lethal addiction" in 1986 (Washton, 1986) even though it was still considered incapable of producing dependence as recently as 1985 (Gawin, 1991). In the period between 1974 and 1985, the national household survey conducted by the National Institute of Drug Abuse, reported the number of individuals who tried cocaine increased 5-fold, from approximately 5 million in 1974 to 25 million in 1985 (Kleber, 1988). Recent trends estimate the volume of use of cocaine to be declining (ONDCP, Sept. 1999).

In an attempt to look at variables that may be related to successful treatment of cocaine and alcohol abusers, a pilot study was completed at a private, outpatient treatment facility (Carise, Forman, Cornely, Mulligan, & Gibbons, 1990). Results showed only 24% of participants whose primary drug of choice was cocaine, completed the full course of treatment, whereas participants whose primary drug of choice was alcohol completed treatment at a rate of 53% (n = 658). Family involvement in treatment showed promise as a predictor of the likelihood that a client will continue in and complete treatment.

Brief Historical Perspectives on Cocaine Abuse

The Incas called the coca leaf a "gift of the sun god" (Kleber, 1988, p. 1360). In the late 1800's Angelo Mariani introduced a popular preparation of coca and wine and was awarded a gold medal and was cited as a benefactor of humanity. During this time period, an Italian neurologist, Paola Mantegazza, described the effects coca had on the physiological state saying "I would rather have a life span of 10 years with coca than one of 1 million centuries without it" (as cited in Kleber, 1988).

In 1884, Freud published *Uber Coca* praising cocaine's ability to increase mood and productivity, and decrease appetite. However, his popularity decreased, and by 1886 Freud was attacked for releasing what peers called the third scourge of mankind. Still, during this time the Coca Cola company was formed, marketing soda containing cocaine and caffeine. The Coca Cola company reported the soda was a headache remedy and a tonic for easily tired people.

In 1906, the Pure Food and Drug Act's labeling regulations led to the elimination of cocaine from most medicines and soft drinks marking the end of easy distribution of cocaine. The 1960's brought a renewed interest in drugs of all kinds including cocaine. This interest continued into the '70s and '80s. During this time period, celebrity endorsements, as well as the media, played significant roles in the popularization of cocaine. J. J. Cale's song "Cocaine" hit the top of billboard charts, and "User's Guides" to cocaine, including guides of how to test for purity, were sold at local bookstores. Robin Williams added his comical thoughts about cocaine use to his performances stating that cocaine was "God's way of telling you you're making too much money."

A leveling off of cocaine use was apparent in the early 1980's as the country learned, again, of its harmful effects. However, this initial decline in cocaine use was nullified by the development of crack cocaine in 1984 and by the circulation of cocaine to lower socioeconomic groups. This new cocaine, crack, reflected a change in route of administration that resulted in an alteration of reinforcing effects and had a strong impact on the progression of the cocaine problem in this country. Over a course of just four years, 1983 to 1987, the cocaine epidemic changed faces. The new cocaine user is less likely to be college educated, more likely to use crack or freebase cocaine than intranasal cocaine, and less likely to be employed (Herridge & Gold,

1988). It is with this cocaine abuser that current treatment strategies tend to fall short of success.

Effects of Alcohol and Drug Abuse on the Family

Approximately ten percent of adult drinkers in America are likely to experience alcoholism or problem drinking at some point in their lives (DeLuca, 1981). Today, many alcoholics continue to live in families that are intact, and many continue to function, albeit marginally, in the workplace. Alcoholism involves sequela that affects the entire family. Drinking problems typically disrupt the economic stability of the family and cause conflict between and among family members. Alcoholism creates a pattern of crisis to which the family adapts (Kaufman & Pattison, 1981).

Alcoholics Anonymous acknowledged the effects of alcohol on the family more than fifty years ago, however, professionals in the substance abuse field did not begin to incorporate alcoholic families into treatment until 1960. Alcoholism counselors were slow to incorporate family needs into treatment, and family therapists had been slow to incorporate alcohol-related problems in their treatment. Historically, alcohol counselors tended to treat the individuals, without attention to the family dynamics involved, and family therapists tended to treat the alcoholic family like any other, not addressing the alcohol problem (Ewing & Fox, 1968).

In recent years, the fields of substance abuse treatment and family therapy have learned from each other, and have begun to adjust the focus of treatment. There is an awareness that the treatment approach needs to be multifaceted, and must continue to take into consideration that addiction and alcoholism are not experienced by an individual in isolation. The individual is part of a family, and the disease effects and is affected by each family member.

The therapists working with these families need a knowledge of substance abuse and its effects on the family as well as extensive experience and knowledge regarding family therapy. Intervention in the addicted family, by family therapy, appears to have the highest potential for success in treatment.

Family Therapy with Substance Abusers

Kaufman (1985) asserts that knowledge of substance abuse problems, its effects on the family, and knowledge of the family as a system are the most necessary ingredients for successful family therapy with substance abusers. The treatment paradigm utilized can be behavioral, holistic, structural, strategic, psychodynamic, or any eclectic combination of these approaches. There is no evidence that any particular treatment approach has an increased effectiveness (Steinglass, 1987).

In a study completed in 1985, Kaufmann reported that some family factors could predict better functioning after treatment. These factors include: (a) greater cohesion and involvement in recreational pursuits; (b) decreased conflict, control, and disagreement; and (c) an increased number of tasks performed by both spouses. Kaufman emphasizes clinicians must keep in mind they are dealing with more than one individual, and differences are multiplied exponentially (1985). Treatment providers must consider all variables for each family member. The substance abusing and non-abusing family member(s) must be considered individually, with attention to possible biological, psychological, and social factors influencing them. This makes the family inherently more difficult to treat.

Even so, the Second Special Report to the U.S. Congress on Alcohol and Health noted family therapy to be the most notable recent advance in psychotherapy for the treatment of alcoholism (Steinglass, 1976). In a study by Moos and Moos (1984) recovered alcoholics (n = 54) and their spouses reported fewer arguments, performed more joint household tasks, and showed higher agreement about their reports than control group families (n = 105) or relapsed alcoholic families (n = 51). Families of recovering alcoholics functioned as well as families of controls. Families of relapsed patients showed lower levels of cohesion, expressiveness, and recreational orientation.

METHODS

Based on clinical experience, as well as this review of the literature, it seemed valuable to look at several variables in substance abuse treatment and their effects on treatment completion and outcome. Therefore, a study examining these variables was completed at an intensive outpatient substance abuse rehabilitation center. One variable studied, thought to decrease the likelihood of treatment completion, was drug of choice. Additionally, the level of involvement of the family in treatment was thought to increase the likelihood of treatment completion and explored.

Subjects

Two hundred and thirty-eight subjects who received treatment in an intensive outpatient program in Philadelphia participated in this study in an intent-to-treat design (n = 238). One hundred and fifteen (48%) of the subjects completed treatment, whereas 123 (52%) subjects received varying amounts of treatment, but did not complete the full course.

The sample consisted of 190 (80%) males and 48 (20%) females (n = 238). Sixty-five percent (n = 156) of the subjects were black, 33% (n = 78) were white, and 1.6% (n = 4) of the sample was representative of other ethnic groups. All subjects met the Diagnostic Statistical Manual III-Revised (DSM III-R) criteria for substance abuse or dependence. One hundred and nine (46%) met the DSM III-R criteria for alcohol dependence, whereas 103 individuals (43%) met the criteria for cocaine dependence. Eleven percent of this sample (n = 26) met criteria of abuse or dependence for other substances such as heroin or marijuana, or met criteria for more than one category.

Greater than half of the subjects had received prior treatment for substance abuse or dependence. Eighty-six subjects (36%) had participated in one prior treatment for substance abuse, whereas 52 subjects (22%) had participated in two or more prior treatments. One hundred (42%) of the subjects had never received prior treatment for substance abuse or dependence (see Table 1).

Upon admission to the treatment program, each participant signed a "Participant's Bill of Rights" including an informed consent to treatment. At discharge, each participant completed a Continuing Care Plan, including an informed consent regarding follow-up assessment.

Measures

To be included in this study, the subject must receive an evaluation, be deemed appropriate for intensive outpatient treatment, and complete the admission process by attending at least one full intensive treatment session.

Discharge Status (Treatment Completion). A participant's progress through treatment and status at discharge is not based predominantly on the number of sessions attended since the number of treatment

TABLE 1. Subject Demographic Information

	n	%
Gender		
Male	190	(80%)
Female	48	(20%)
Ethnicity		
White	78	(33%)
Black	156	(65%)
Other	4	(2%)
Drug of Choice		
Alcohol	109	(46%)
Cocaine	103	(43%)
Other	26	(11%)
Prior Treatment		
None	100	(42%)
One	86	(36%)
Two or More	52	(22%)

sessions attended is not a reliable measure of treatment success. Therefore, data were collected on the level of discharge status and divided into five categories as described below.

Individuals admitted into the intensive outpatient treatment program who attended less than five sessions in total, were considered to have not fully engaged in the treatment program. Attendance at less than five sessions would indicate duration of involvement in treatment for less than two weeks. A clinical decision was made to characterize subjects who attended treatment for less than two weeks as never fully engaging in the treatment experience. These subjects were categorized as "Did Not Engage" and accounted for 19% of the sample (n = 45). This category does not include individuals who transferred to an alternate level of care.

Subjects who did engage in treatment (by attending at least five sessions), but who did not continue to complete treatment, received a discharge status of "Did Not Complete" (DNC). This represented a total of 29% of the sample (n = 68); these subjects completed varying lengths of treatment ranging from 5 to 33 sessions. They may have left treatment for any one of a variety of reasons (e.g., treatment interfering with work schedule, belief they could maintain sobriety without treatment, relocation to another area, change of employment not requiring treatment), however, this category does not include individuals who left treatment due to transfer to an alternate level of care.

Subjects who attended this treatment program must achieve numerous goals to be recognized as "treatment completers." To qualify as having completed treatment, subjects must (a) remain drug and alcohol free for a minimum of 60 days; (b) complete Weekend Recovery Plans; (c) complete a Psychosocial History Questionnaire; and (d) complete a Continuing Care Plan. Completion of treatment was operationally defined as the aforementioned in this paragraph, participation in a graduation ceremony, and receipt of a certificate of completion. One hundred and fifteen (48%) of the subjects were "treatment completers."

Subjects, who began intensive outpatient treatment but are subsequently referred to an alternate level of care because they required inpatient treatment, are represented by the "Transferred Inpatient" category. Anyone who transferred to an inpatient facility, regardless of the number of sessions engaged in, was categorized as a transfer inpatient.

Subjects, who began intensive outpatient treatment but subsequently transferred to a more traditional, non-intensive outpatient treatment, are represented by the "Transferred Outpatient" category regardless of the number of sessions attended.

Transfers to both inpatient and outpatient facilities accounted for only 4% (n = 10) of the sample. Due to the small number of subjects in these groups, subjects who transferred to other facilities for continued treatment were excluded from analysis. This exclusion criterion was deemed necessary since the hypotheses in this study centered primarily on subject's completion or failure to complete treatment.

Drug of Choice. Data collected on Drug of Choice was initially divided into fourteen categories. Whereas it is understood that most subjects in substance abuse treatment generally use a variety of drugs, most also indicate a clear preference for a specific drug; this was called the "primary drug of choice." In this study, the subject's drug of choice was defined by several measures.

Firstly, each participant specified "drug of choice" during the evaluation and intake session. Every participant who entered into intensive treatment first participated in an evaluation and intake with the clinical director of the center. At that time, an intake form is completed. Included in the evaluation, and recorded on the intake form, are records of the substances used by the participant, listed in order of preference. Also recorded at that time is a diagnosis according to the DSM-III-R assigned to the participant by the clinical director. In addition, after the third treatment session, the participant completes a psychosocial evaluation. There is a section of this evaluation where the participant records again the most used substance. To be categorized as having a specific drug of choice, the participant's data must be consistent across these three assessments. That is, self-report upon intake, diagnosis, and self-report after the third session, in the psychosocial history form, must all indicate the same drug of choice.

Initially, data on drug of choice was collected in 14 categories (i.e.: alcohol categories; beer, wine, or liquor, cocaine categories; intranasal users, crack or freebase, marijuana, heroin, barbiturates, amphetamines, etc.). However, after data collection, categories were collapsed. Alcohol (beer, wine, and liquor) accounted for 46% of participants drug of choice (n = 109), whereas cocaine (used intranasally, intravenously, or smoked) accounted for 43% of participants' drug of choice (n = 103). The remaining categories: marijuana, heroin, other opiates, sleeping pills, tranquilizers, angel dust, others, and no drug of choice were condensed because these categories amounted to only 11% (n = 26) of the sample. Eleven subjects (4.6%) could not be classified into a single drug of choice, 5 subjects (2%) were primarily marijuana abusers, and 3 subjects (1%) used predominantly opiates other than heroin.

Due to the potential analytic confound that users of drugs other than alcohol or cocaine present to the clarity of this study, and not withstanding the small proportion represented by these subjects, data from subjects who were not classified as either primary alcohol abusers or primary cocaine abusers, were deleted from the analysis.

Family Involvement. The concept measured was the general level of involvement on the part of the family. For the purposes of this study, individuals involved in committed relationships with participants, although not legally related to them, were considered family members regardless of legal or cohabitation status.

The treatment program included participation in group sessions specifically designed for the substance abuser and their family member(s). It occurred weekly, on Saturdays, from 9:30 a.m. until 12:30 p.m. Each time a subject brought an adult family member(s) with them to a Saturday multiple family group, this was counted as participation of the family. A total of 121 of the subjects (59%) did not have any family member involvement in any type of sessions. For those families who were involved, most attended one time (19% of the total sample, n = 38). Those families accounting for 2 or 3 visits made up 12% of the total sample (n = 25), whereas 9% attended more than 3 sessions.

Data Collection. The project director documented information on these variables (client discharge, drug of choice, family member participation). Collection of these data did not depend on maintaining contact with the client; therefore, these data were obtainable for all subjects.

Treatment Program. The treatment program is an outpatient drug and alcohol rehabilitation program that is part of a non-profit hospital. The program provides varying levels of substance abuse and dependence treatment, including traditional outpatient therapy, family therapy, court stipulated drunk driving programs, and intensive outpatient treatment. Completing the intensive outpatient treatment program takes approximately two months and consists of two phases. In Phase One, participants attend treatment from 6:00 p.m. until 10:30 p.m. three evenings each week, and from 9:30 a.m. until 12:30 p.m. on Saturdays. In the second phase of treatment, participants continue to attend Saturdays from 9:30 a.m. until 12:30 p.m., but attend only two other evenings each week.

Each evening treatment session consists of an initial group therapy session that lasts approximately two hours, from 6 p.m. until 8 p.m. Following this, the participants go, as a group, to a nearby Alcoholics Anonymous (AA) meeting. The group returns at approximately 9:30 p.m. and participates in a discussion about the meeting and/or a didactic session about alcoholism and drug abuse problems.

The portion of the treatment program that meets on Saturday is a multiple family group session. This involves participants from both Phase One and Phase Two and their family members or significant others. The family program is a 9-week course consisting of nine different didactic and experiential sessions. Treatment participants are required to attend the family program even if they cannot bring a family member.

Of 238 subjects entered into the study, 26 were excluded because they did not fit into a designated drug of choice or had a primary drug of choice other than alcohol or cocaine. A total of 8 subjects were excluded because they transferred out of intensive outpatient treatment. Therefore, data included a total sample of 204 subjects where 105 (51%) were primary alcohol abusers and 99 (49%) were primary cocaine abusers (see Table 2).

A 2 × 3 chi-square analysis (drug of choice by level of treatment completion) revealed the groups differed significantly regarding level of treatment completion, $\chi^2(2, n = 204) = 6.63, p = .036$. The primary alcohol abuse group had a statistically higher rate of treatment completion in comparison to the primary cocaine abusers. A Cramer's V statistic for 2 × 3 chi-square was computed and revealed the strength of relationship between alcohol and cocaine-abusing groups with regard to treatment completion was statistically significant (Cramer's $V = .18, p < .05$).

A second analysis was performed, generating Gamma statistics for the primary alcohol abusing group and the primary cocaine-abusing group. This analysis examined the impact of family involvement on completion of treatment. The Gamma statistic was used to reflect additional information available from the ranking dimension of the variables, a relationship not considered using nominal measures. This analysis revealed a significant relationship between family involvement and treatment completion (see Table 3), for the alcohol-abusing group ($g = .58, z = 2.8, p < .01$).

The cocaine-abusing group also showed a significant relationship between family involvement and discharge status ($g = .44, z = 2.11, p < .05$). Family involvement in treatment appears to increase the likelihood that a subject will continue in and complete treatment, regardless of the subject's drug of choice.

TABLE 2. Discharge Status by Drug of Choice

Discharge Status	Drug Of Choice	
	Alcohol	Cocaine
Did Not Engage	16 (7.8%)	25 (12.3%)
Did Not Complete	26 (12.7%)	32 (15.7%)
Completed Treatment	63 (30.9%)	42 (20.6%)
Totals	105 (51%)	99 (49%)

TABLE 3. Gamma Statistics for Family Involvement

	Alcohol Group	Cocaine Group
Discharge Status	.58**	.44*

*p < .05   **p < .01

Limitations of the Study

Data records on demographic variables such as gender and ethnicity are easily kept and could prove useful when evaluating efficacy of the program among different groups of individuals, however, this study's importance is circumscribed by the belief that an individual who enters into and completes the full course of treatment, is most likely to remain abstinent from drugs and alcohol. A follow-up study of these patients (those who do and those who do not complete treatment) could have provided additional valuable information.

This study could have been made more interesting if data had been recorded on the participant's educational level and age. Evaluation of variables such as these contributes rudimentary data for analysis and can provide valuable information. Evaluation of demographic variables such as these can be the first step in guiding treatment providers towards making changes that will increase the efficacy of treatment.

Implications for Involvement of Family

Data analysis showed a significant increase in treatment completion when the family was involved. This significance was found for both primary cocaine abusers and primary alcohol abusers. Much literature is available on family and marital therapy of substance abusers, however, there is a paucity of research evaluating the effect of family involvement on treatment completion. This study reinforces the value of family involvement in treatment; therefore it seems beneficial to review the current literature on marital and family treatment of substance abusers.

Family Therapy in the Treatment of Alcoholism. The limitations of evaluating family treatment of alcoholics are extensive. They include: small sample sizes, lack of comparison groups, difficult outcome measures, utilization of diverse therapies, and difficulty factoring out extraneous variables. However, a number of researchers have reported positive results utilizing family therapy in the treatment of alcoholics (Anderson & Henderson, 1983). Kaufman (1985) compared paid family therapy, unpaid family therapy, paid family "movie treatment," and non-family treatment. He conducted a 1-year post-treatment follow-up. Results indicated the two family therapy treatments produced much better outcomes (as measured by abstinence), than the non-family treatments. The non-family treatment and the movie groups did not differ from each other. Three studies were completed (Scopetta, King, Szapocznik, & Tillman, 1979; Stanton, 1980; and Wunderlich, Lozes, & Lewis 1974) showing family treatment to be superior to other modes of treatment.

Anderson and Henderson (1983) report education to be an important part of family treatment of alcoholism. They point out that treatment should teach the spouse to accept alcoholism as a disease, that they did not cause it and are not responsible for curing it. This has long been a part of non-professional self-help groups such as Al-Anon and Al-Ateen. Instruction and education is not an end in itself, however, it can help the family to feel less responsible for the illness. Boyer (1989) states the therapist should emphasize the disease concept in an effort to minimize blame and should praise the family for having the courage to work on the illness. Finally, two other very interesting and promising modalities of treatment that involve families are becoming popular in substance abuse centers. They are multiple couples and multiple family group therapies.

Multiple Couples and Multiple Family Therapy in Treatment of Alcoholism. This unique form of therapy is showing increasing success and popularity in the treatment of substance abuse. This approach involves group therapy techniques and knowledge of group process as well as knowledge of family issues and the effects of alcoholism on the family relationships. Multiple couples groups usually meet weekly and involve 4 to 7 couples. The spouses can meet conjointly or concurrently. That is, the alcoholics of the groups may meet for group therapy, while at the same time, the spouses meet for education and group therapy with another therapist. The most innovative technique involves the couples meeting conjointly.

Conjoint multiple couples group involves therapy emphasizing experiences of all members of the group. Patterns of difficulty with communication between and among married partners are explored. A group member who may find it difficult to tell their spouse how drinking affects them may find it easier to tell another member's spouse. The different ways of coping with alcoholism as well as the different ways of coping with sobriety are shared among the couples.

A study completed in an alcoholism treatment center involving 20 couples participating in multiple couples group and 20 couples without multiple couples group, was done by Cadogan (cited in Zimberg, 1982). These couples were matched for sociodemographic characteristics, severity of alcoholism, and previous treatment history. At a 6-month follow-up, the rate of improvement was significantly greater among the alcoholic couples that received multiple couples therapy in comparison with those who did not.

In another study, Gallant et al. (cited in Zimberg, 1982), followed 118 couples that received multiple couples therapy in an outpatient treatment facility. The results stated 45% of the couples experienced significant improvement in the marital relationship.

Similar to multiple-couples therapy, some treatment centers are now offering multiple-family group therapy. This generally consists of several patients on an inpatient unit who may be involved in daily group therapy together. This group of patients and their family members form a larger group for multiple family therapy (MFT). This group may include older adult alcoholics and their adult children, adolescent alcoholics and their parents, as well as the adult alcoholic who may bring both his parents and his own children into the treatment.

Often it is observed that relatives of the alcoholic will find it less difficult to tell someone else how alcoholism has hurt their family, than telling their alcoholic family member. Hendricks (1971) found at one-year follow-up, individuals who received MFT were twice as likely to remain in continuous therapy than addicts not receiving MFT. The Kaufman's work (Kaufman & Kaufman, 1981) has shown that adolescent addicts who participate in MFT have half the recidivism rate of those who do not.

Well designed studies are still needed to evaluate the efficacy of family involvement in substance abuse treatment, however, there seems to be considerable indication that many different types of family therapy can be beneficial in the treatment of substance abusers.

CONCLUSIONS

Two hundred and four subjects participated in this study, 105 primary alcohol abusers, and 99 primary cocaine abusers. The cocaine abusers had a significantly lower rate of treatment completion in comparison to alcohol abusers. Treatment centers are obliged to work on increasing efficacy of treatment for these subjects. The particular needs of this subgroup should be evaluated in an effort to provide more satisfactory treatment.

Two variables were discovered that appear to increase the likelihood of treatment completion. Family involvement in treatment had a significant effect on both the alcohol and the cocaine abusing groups, increasing the likelihood that individuals from either group would continue in and complete treatment.

This study supports the value of continuing to provide family therapy to substance abusers. Future research should seek to replicate this finding, as well as expand studies to evaluate the impact of family involvement on continued recovery. The role of the family in the treatment of substance abusers cannot be underestimated.

REFERENCES

Anderson, S., & Henderson, D. (1983). Family therapy in the treatment of alcoholism. *Social Work in Health Care, 8*(4), 79-94.

Boyer, P.A. (1989). A guide to therapy with families with a chemically dependent parent. *Psychotherapy, 26*(1), 88-95.

Carise, D., Forman, R., Cornely, W., Mulligan, F., & Gibbons, T. (1990). [Rehab After Work Outcome Study, 1988-1990]. Unpublished raw data.

DeLuca, J.R. (Ed.) (1981). *Alcohol and Health.* Rockville, MD: National Institute of Alcohol Abuse and Alcoholism.

Ewing, J., & Fox, R. (1968). Family therapy of alcoholism. *Current Psychiatric Therapies, 8*, 86-91.

Freud, S. (1884). Uber coca. *Zentralbl Ther, 2*, 289-314.

Gawin, F. (1991). Cocaine addiction: Psychology and neurophysiology. *Science, 251*, 1580-1585.

Hendricks, W. (1971). Use of multifamily counseling groups in treatment of male narcotic addicts. *International Journal of Group Psychotherapy, 21*, 34-90.

Herridge, P., & Gold, M.S. (1988). The new user of cocaine: Evidence from *800-CO-CAINE. Psychiatric Annals, 19*, 521-522.

Kaufman, E. (1985). Family systems and family therapy of substance abuse: An overview of two decades of research and clinical experience. *The International Journal of the Addictions, 20*, 897-916.

Kaufman, E. & Kaufman, P. (1981). Multiple family therapy: A new direction in the treatment of drug abusers. *American Journal of Drug and Alcohol Abuse, 4*, 467-478.

Kaufman, E. & Pattison, E. (1981). Differential methods of family therapy in the treatment of alcoholism. *Journal of Studies on Alcohol, 42*, 951-971.

Kleber, H. (1988). Epidemic cocaine abuse: America's present, Britain's future? *British Journal of Addiction, 83*, 1359-1371.

Moos, R., & Moos, B. (1984). The process of recovery from alcoholism: III. Comparing functioning families of alcoholics and matched control families. *Journal of Studies on Alcohol, 45*, 111-118.

Office of National Drug Control Policy (Sept. 1999). Data Snapshot: Drug Abuse in American, 1999. Unpublished manuscript.

Pettinati, H. (1990). *Economic costs of drug & alcohol abuse.* Paper presented at conference on substance abuse treatment, Carrier Foundation, Belle Mead, NJ.

Scopetta, M., King, O., Szapocznik, J., & Tillman, M. (1979) Ecological structural family therapy with Cuban immigrant families. Unpublished, 1979, as cited in Stanton, 1979.

Stanton, M. (1980). Some overlooked aspects of the family and drug abuse. In B.G. Ellis (ed). *Drug Abuse from the Family Perspective.* Rockville, MD: NIDA, DHEW.

Steinglass, P. (1976). Experimenting with family treatment approaches to alcoholism, a review 1950-75. *Family Process*, 15, 97-123.

Steinglass, P. (1987). *The Alcoholic Family*, New York: Basic Books.

Washton, A.M. (1986). "Crack": The newest lethal addiction. *Medical Aspects of Human Sexuality*, Sept. 1986, 49-51.

Wunderlich, R., Lozes, J., & Lewis, J. (1974). Recidivism rates of group therapy participants and other adolescents processed by juvenile court. *Psychotherapy: Theory, Research & Practice, 11 (3).* <sic> 61, 243-245.

Zimberg, S. (1982). Office psychotherapy of alcoholism. In Solomon, J. (Ed.), *Alcoholism and Clinical Psychiatry.* New York: Plenum Medical Company.

Index